elcome to

Northwest
Forest

Bud Hadfield

E.M. SCHIWETZ

Wealth
Within Reach

Wealth
Within Reach

Bud Hadfield

Cypress Publishing
Cypress, Texas

Library of Congress Cataloging-in-Publication Data:

Hadfield, Bud, 1923-
    Wealth Within Reach/Bud Hadfield.
        p.   cm.
    ISBN 0-9645102-1-9
    1. Success in business—United States—Case studies. 2. Kwik Kopy Corporation—History. 3. Hadfield, Bud, 1923-
        I. Title.
    HF5386.H213   1992
    338.7'6862'097641411—dc20   92-25858
                                                            CIP

56789 MVP 98765

Printed in the United States of America

1st Edition   1992
2nd Edition   1994
3rd Edition   1995
4th Edition   1998
5th Edition   2000
6th Edition   2003
7th Edition   2005

To my wife, Mary, who named Kwik Kopy,
my children, Jimmy and Kathy,
and my Kwik Kopy family . . .
all several thousand of them.

Contents

Foreword

This is a book about a company that made it big. And fast. And came within an inch of losing everything.

The story goes far beyond the examples in recent vogue, that is, the twenty-three-year-old who lands in *Inc. Magazine* as a superhero one year and a bum the next. At the age of forty-four, after failing in a series of other ventures, I started a company called Kwik Kopy Franchise Corporation.

Unlike the mythical fellow who wanted to invent a soft drink, tried six times and quit (which is why you never heard of Six-Up), I wouldn't stop. Rebounding from failure is a topic I refer to often in the coming pages and with good reason. Failure is a learning experience. It can be a gravestone or a stepping stone.

We all have the talent to fail. Some are better at it than others. But all failures are temporary until you accept one of them as permanent.

By doing some things right, I found myself a multimillionaire within a few years. By making a wrong turn or two, and a major error, I darn near blew it all. Kwik Kopy will never be a General Motors, and Bud Hadfield will never be a Lee Iacocca (and I don't want to be). I am living the wondrous life of a man who made it and, even more important, I'm happy.

At eighty-two, I am often asked when I plan to retire. The answer is *never*. It's pure joy to run your own business. I love it. I love the people around me.

There are several can't-miss ways to personal success. They are in the book. Find them. Make them yours.

9

Acknowledgments

Every book is in some respect a team effort, and this one is no exception. I owe a special debt to those who contributed their time, ideas, and special talents in assembling the product you hold in your hands.

Many gave interviews that appear in the following pages. Others offered support and encouragement. My special thanks are owed to the following: Mary Hadfield, Nath Winfield, Andrea Nevarez, Bob Harrison, Pattie Paddy, Steve Hammerstein, Charlie Porting, and Nancy McCoy. Their contributions and efforts are greatly appreciated.

A final thanks to my good friend Mickey Herskowitz, an excellent writer, who guided me through these pages.

Bud Hadfield

Prologue

Many, if not most of us, would like to lead our lives with the energy and honesty and fullness of Dr. Norman Vincent Peale—if only we had the time. He was one of those rare souls, a ninety-four-year-old man who still had potential.

Motivator, minister, author, Dr. Peale was one of the principal speakers at the Twenty-Second Annual Kwik Kopy International Conference in Houston in September of 1990. I will not dwell here on all the meanings of that sentence, nor the pleasure and amazement they inspire in me: that there *is* an international Kwik Kopy, that we have successfully held twenty-two conferences, and that we have attracted speakers of the stature of Dr. Peale.

Our theme for the annual conference was "Up Where We Belong," and artfully, and often, Dr. Peale weaved it into his remarks. The next morning, as we were driving to the airport, he repeated the phrase and said, "Wouldn't that make a wonderful title for a book?" Then he stopped and looked off into space for a moment. Suddenly, he threw up his arms and hollered (there is no other way to put it): "No! Up Where *You* Belong. Yes, that's it. Now *that* would make a fine title for a book."

Dr. Peale had no way of knowing, and I was too timid to tell him, that I was in fact writing a book about the company I had founded with such modest goals in the late 1960s. That company had brought us to this time and place. The last thing I wanted was for Dr. Peale to think we had taken liberties with his generous nature. But as chance

• • • • • • • • • • • • • • • • • • • •

I found Dr. Peale to be an
extraordinary man,
religious without the
impression of piety, wise
without the impression
of preaching.

• • • • • • • • • • • • • • • • • • • •

would have it, we had reached the same conclusion. This variation of our theme spoke so directly to the soaring spirit in each of us that I had already decided to adopt it as part of the title.

Still, our eminent guest had given voice to the words. My version existed on an ink-stained cocktail napkin. Would it appear that we had lifted his idea with no acknowledgment? That morning I felt I had to say something. So very carefully, I said, "Dr. Peale, it happens that I have been working on a book and looking for a title for a long time. I was going to write you and ask for your suggestions. But now that we're here, talking together..."

It wasn't necessary to finish the sentence. He looked at me, broke into a big smile and said, "That's what the title of your book should be. It's a good title, Bud. Go ahead and use it." In the end, as happens in publishing, there was an editorial compromise. "Up Where You Belong" became the subtitle. Still, the point is unchanged. His gesture reminded me once more of the total unselfishness of this man who so willingly shares of himself, as he and his wife crisscross our country, speaking to tens of thousands of people every year. (And at an age where, as Casey Stengel once said, not many people are still breathing.)

I found Dr. Peale to be an extraordinary man, religious without the impression of piety, wise without the impression of preaching. An old friend of mine gave the invocation at our annual banquet, a retired Baptist preacher named Dr. Roy Ladd. He had alerted me to a question he planned to ask Dr. Peale, and I wasn't entirely comfortable with its appropriateness.

The moment they met, I saw that they understood each other as theologians. Ladd looked at the famed minister and said, "Dr. Peale, do you really believe in prayer?"

• • • • • • • • • • • • • • • • • • • •

Long ago I learned never
to give up on a child.
He may have a learning
disability. He might be
hyperactive, or
withdrawn, the product of
an unstable home. But
sometimes, if you try, you
can look right into his
heart and see the lights
come on.

• • • • • • • • • • • • • • • • • • • •

And quick as a finger snap, Dr. Peale laughed and said, "What do you think?"

That was all either of them had to say. Their silence was the equivalent, for most of us, of an hour's conversation on the power of prayer.

They spent the night in Houston, and my friend, Kent Harding, our Canadian licensee, and I walked Dr. Peale and Ruth, his wife of sixty years, to their hotel suite. We bade them good-night, closed the door and were halfway down the hall when I heard his voice call out, "Bud!" I stopped, turned and said, "Yes, Dr. Peale?" His head was leaning out the doorway. "I like you," he sang out, and disappeared again behind the door.

Three little words, but to me they had the sound of trumpets.

I count myself a member of a not very exclusive club: an admirer of Dr. Peale's work and an avid reader of his writings. He has written thirty-six books, and he has the gift that Dale Carnegie had. He doesn't preach. He offers one example after another and lets you draw your own conclusion about how it relates to living.

I thought of this philosophy on a day when I was invited to speak to a special education class at a Houston-area junior high school. The class numbered twenty or twenty-five youngsters of the kind sometimes called "at-risk" students. The odds are that many of them will not graduate from high school.

Long ago I learned never to give up on a child. He may have a learning disability. He may be hyperactive, or withdrawn, the product of an unstable home. But sometimes, if you try, you can look right into his heart and see the lights come on.

• • • • • • • • • • • • • • • • • • • •

I knew, instinctively,
that you do not make a
speech to a roomful of
wary, restless and
distracted kids.

• • • • • • • • • • • • • • • • • • • •

Right in the middle of the front row sat a bright-eyed little black girl of about thirteen, who looked at me with unconcealed suspicion. Her expression said: "What could this well-fed old white guy, this honky, possibly say that would relate to me and my world?"

I knew, instinctively, that you do not make a speech to a roomful of wary, restless and distracted kids. For openers, I said, "Look, you guys, I think you can do things that you don't think you can.

"How many of you have a good memory?"

Not one of them raised a hand. So I looked around the room and picked out ten different items and numbered them — an old word association game. A door, clock, map, flag, waste basket. "Can anyone call them out by number, at random?" I asked. They weren't even interested.

I said, "Well, we're going to do it and you better try. I ran through the numbers—one, run; two, zoo; three, tree; four, door; an old Carnegie technique—and made them repeat it over and over until they were noisy and laughing. Now I had their curiosity. I looked at the little black girl and said, "Give me all ten."

Her look was pure ice. I told her to stand. She stayed in her seat. Slowly, she began to fumble with the answers. She needed a little help along the way, but she did all ten and the class applauded, a simple, unplanned outburst of respect. Her eyes said, "I showed you."

Then I had a teacher in the back of the room hang a picture on ten memory pegs around the room. I reviewed it once, then quizzed my friend on the front row at random. Number 4? Number 8? She answered all ten, at random, and the class went crazy.

• • • • • • • • • • • • • • • • • • • •

This is what I learned in
meeting Dr. Norman
Vincent Peale and from
my encounter with the
bright little girl in the
at-risk class: if the lights
come on, this book has
achieved its purpose.

• • • • • • • • • • • • • • • • • • • •

The look changed. It wasn't yet an "I like you" look. It was something much better. The lights had come on, and for the split seconds that we made contact, I had all I could do to keep my eyes from puddling up.

A few weeks later, the teachers brought the class to our Kwik Kopy campus for a tour. We started the tour by bribing them with a visit to our cafeteria and all the frozen yogurt they could eat, with a variety of toppings. The little girl squeezed her way to the front of the bunch and looked up at me with a great, big smile. I wanted to hug her. Instead, I said, "Give me ten." She zipped right through them.

This is what I learned in meeting Dr. Norman Vincent Peale and from my encounter with the bright little girl in the at-risk class: If the lights come on, this book has achieved its purpose.

The Printer

Without him, tyrants and hum-bugs in all countries would have their own way. He is a friend of intelligence and thought. A friend of liberty, of freedom, of law. Indeed, the friend of every man who is a friend of order.

Of all inventions, of all discoveries in science and art, of all the great results in the wonderful progress of mechanical energy and skill, the Printer is the only product of civilization necessary to the existence of free men.

— Charles Dickens

Co-Author's Note

There are books that propose to tell the ambitious how to succeed and those who are already successful how to build an empire if they only have the time and the credit. So much of what is currently written and taught seems aimed at people who can think only of a "career path," with no sense of contributing to society.

Bud Hadfield founded Kwik Kopy International and saw it become the leader in an industry that deals with a fundamental and timeless set of products. His book is about personal and business survival, about the work ethic, and about dealing with difficult bosses and uninspired co-workers. It is about turning good people loose to test their wings and firing the ones who hold others back. It is about the joys and vagaries of the workplace, and the ones we learn from: family, friends, vendors, employees and competitors.

At the onset of this project, Bud stressed that the book should be motivational and partly a history of the company, not an autobiography. However, casual research established that this was one instruction not easily followed. At every turn, one was reminded that Bud and Kwik Kopy are inseparable. You can't have one without the other.

This is probably the logical place to attempt to describe the man whose ideas jump across the pages to come. To begin with, precious few know and *none* use his given name, Frederick. Nor does he. All of which is understandable. A Frederick is someone who attended Amherst and has lunch at "the club." You can go blind digging through the files at Kwik Kopy, searching for a newsletter or a memorandum or document that refers to him as anything other than Bud Hadfield. There are never any quote marks around the name. His employees, his friends, his lawyers and bankers all know him as Bud. (As in, this Bud's for you.)

He is a large, shambling man, so informal in his attire that a stranger might mistake him for the company mechanic. Rarely is he discovered in the workplace wearing a coat and dress shirt or necktie. In the way he walks and talks and the way he works, he is a cross between Art Carney and Columbo.

For a telling first impression of Bud Hadfield, we recommend to you the experience of his secretary, Andrea Nevarez, who is uncompromising in her loyalty and her objectivity.

Andrea joined Kwik Kopy in September of 1984, having left what was, on paper, a better job with the Houston-based foods division of Coca-Cola. She had developed at least two habits not likely to make an employee very popular with a conservative management. She kept proposing changes, such as sick leave when a child was ill. She clipped articles from *The Wall Street Journal* about companies that adopted new employee benefits and conveniences. Andrea decided her future might be limited the day her boss compared her to Norma Rae, a rebellious factory worker in the 1960s.

Andrea's knowledge of Kwik Kopy consisted of having walked past the window, years earlier, of the only Kwik Kopy center in the small Pennsylvania town where she lived. "In Houston I saw an ad in a newspaper," she says, "secretary to a vice-chairman. I called and set up an interview. You know how you get a feeling when you go into a place? Either you like it, or you don't. I had been interviewed at an engineering firm, and it was so cold and quiet, I knew I couldn't work there.

"When I went to Kwik Kopy, the receptionist was Gloria Palmer, a good ole girl, one of those people who makes you feel right at home. And basically that was what attracted me to Kwik Kopy; it was a warm, friendly place where I thought I would be happy."

She went to work for Joe Lambert, the company's treasurer and vice-chairman. Bud was out of town on an annual company retreat in the backwoods of Canada. He returned at the end of the month.

This is not an attempt to put down a legendary company for the purpose of praising a smaller one. But whatever the size, most companies develop their own culture—which brings us back to Bud Hadfield.

"I didn't know this at the time," says Andrea, "but when he has been gone on a long trip he likes to make the rounds and say hello to everybody.

"At Coca-Cola, you didn't interact with upper management. You might nod if you passed the president of the foods division in the hall, but you didn't stop and have a chat with him. When Bud stopped at my desk, I just stared. He was wearing a jump suit. He still had a beard of three weeks' growth. I think I said one word, 'Hello.'

"He went back to his office and told LaDonna Meadows, who was then his administrative assistant, that he didn't like me. He said, 'Joe Lambert's new secretary is a real snot. I don't like her at all.' "

When Bud's secretary turned in her notice a few months later, he offered the job to Andrea Nevarez. That's

Bud Hadfield. "We are both blunt people," Andrea says. "I asked about the salary and he wouldn't discuss it. He said, 'If you want the job you'll come to work for me because you want to, not because of the money.' I was saying to myself, 'Is he crazy? I'm not supposed to think about the money?' It was the first thing on my mind.

"I went home and thought, I don't know if I should take the job or not. People in the company kept telling me, you don't want to work for him. Even the man I worked for said, 'Think about it. He can be difficult.' I didn't know he had gone through four or five secretaries in three years. They were taking bets down in marketing that I wouldn't last six months. It was a riot. Then I thought, if I don't take the job someone else will, and if it turns out to be a good situation I'm going to kick myself for not taking a chance. And being a typical, hard-headed Italian, with everyone telling me not to do something, I decided I would do it.

"Then I started to work for him. Even his ex-secretary took me to lunch and tried to talk me out of it. He had a temper then. He has mellowed in the last six or seven years. He would kill me if he heard me say that, but he has. Back then, I could be halfway down the hall and hear him chew someone out—with the door closed. Sometimes he would ask me to call ten people into his office, and I knew what was going to happen. I used to feel so bad telling them, 'Bud would like to see you.' I didn't even want to look at them as they went by."

Yet the explosive boss and the emotional secretary, in her word, "meshed." It helped that she could take a joke. "I was blunt," she said, "and he could accept that. He liked the fact that he could tease me and make me the butt of his jokes. It didn't bother me, and it was good for him. I could roll with it. With Bud you can be yourself."

Eventually they cleared the air about that icy first meeting. "I explained that at Coca-Cola you didn't routinely talk to the executives. He found this interesting because it reinforced his belief in what he didn't want Kwik Kopy to be. He doesn't like that corporate image where people don't feel like they're a part of the team, where there is a management level and a lower level and they don't mix. With Bud, they mix."

The story is repeated here not only as a character study, but because it illustrates a point. This is the way real people function inside a real company. They argue, adjust, cope, rise above their doubts, lift each other up.

"At first, I was hesitant to argue with him," Andrea confided. If he was in a bad mood or had lost his temper, I knew it would be fruitless because I would lose. I had seen him operate with other people. I told him, 'If you ever holler at me, I'm going to do one of two things. I will either cry or holler back.' He just laughed. In seven years he has never raised his voice to me. But once or twice when I was mad or frustrated, I cried. On these occasions he would yank tissues out of the box and sail them at me, saying they cost a nickel a tissue and warn me not to drip tears on his desk. He is totally uncomfortable with tears."

On another occasion, Andrea went two days without talking to her boss. She brought him his coffee, avoiding his eyes, and left the room. "I kind of ignored him, and it was getting me no place. Finally, I stopped in his doorway and said, 'I guess you're not even interested in knowing why I'm mad at you?'

"He said, 'Oh, yeah. I know you're mad, and I know why.'

"I said, 'Well, aren't you going to say anything?'

" 'No,' he said, 'you've been walking stiff-legged for two days, and I figured you would get around to bringing it up.' " Her laugh was one of resignation. "He just takes anger away from you," she said, "and I could smack him for doing that to me."

"He is a good judge of character," says Andrea. "He has an unbelievable mind for retaining information. He understands finance better than the accountants. He understands the law, sometimes, better than the lawyers. He can visualize things other people can't see."

So we return to an essential point about Bud Hadfield: His gruffness is often used to conceal a soft heart. He can be among the most considerate of men, a tireless sender of notes.

I received one of his notes while we were editing his manuscript, even though I saw him with some frequency. He had circled a quote from Mickey Mantle that appeared in the sports column I write for *The Houston Post*.

Mantle had figured out that between his career strikeouts and walks, he had played the equivalent of seven seasons without hitting the ball.

Bud's note said: "Great quote. I can use this." He will save that quote on an index card or a writing tablet until he needs to make a point about success and failure and keeping things in perspective. But something more subtle was involved in his gesture. He appreciated Mantle's modesty, and he let me know that he was reading my work.

This is Bud at his best, turning friendship into readership, sending out soft strokes. In the process, he squirreled away a thought for the winter.

Mickey Herskowitz

In 1998, Andrea Nevarez married and settled into a new nest. I was as overjoyed for her as I was overwhelmed by the daunting challenge of finding someone to replace her.

I happened to read one of my favorite lectures, "Acres of Diamonds," by Dr. Russell H. Conwell, recounting the legend of a landowner who sold his farm and left his family to roam the continents in search of a diamond mine. In the course of his journey, he became destitute and despondent. He plunged into the tides, never to be seen again.

Meanwhile, back at the ranch... the new landowner had discovered a curious stone in the riverbed, which he placed on his mantel. One day a visitor, spying the stone, asked if the old farmer had returned, because indeed there was a diamond on the mantel. Closer inspection revealed acres of diamonds scarcely concealed throughout the land. This was the discovery of the magnificent diamond mines of Golconda. Right there under the nose of the man who left them to search the globe for diamonds.

Inspired by the lecture, I noticed Debbie Clifford, who joined our family in 1987. As Steve Hammerstein's executive assistant since 1991, I had seen her perform miracles so often that I'd become as blind as the Golconda farmer. Determined not to repeat his mistake, I was able to persuade Steve to allow Debbie to also serve as my assistant.

Over the years we've gotten to know each other well. She's one of the most stubborn women I know and when I tell her so - she thanks me. I wouldn't trade her for all the diamonds in the world!

Today, Debbie Clifford is a vice president of ICED and contributes to our efforts at the very highest levels. Most importantly to me, she saves my life at least ten times a day. Thank you, Debbie!

You can read Dr. Conwell's lecture, "Acres of Diamonds," at http://www.temple.edu/ about/temples_founder/acres_text.html

Chapter

1

The Printer's Helper

There is no intention here of glorifying failure. There is far too much of it going around lately, and the American nature doesn't sanction the words "I give up." But I have known failure and learned from it—more than once.

I had my own print shop in the basement of my home in Cranston, Rhode Island, when I was a student in junior high school. I published a newspaper, *The Family News*, sold ads, and went door to door to take small orders for stationery and business cards. Although the future was unclear to me then and for many years to come, I believe I was born to be an entrepreneur, as some are born to be lawyers or left fielders.

An incident that surely helped shape my life occurred when I was thirteen or fourteen, just before summer vacation. The printing teacher at the junior high, Mr. Gage, said, "I know you have a print shop at home. Would you happen to have a job for me this summer?"

The request echoed in my mind. Here was a college graduate, a teacher, asking a teenager, one of his students, for employment. Did this somehow call into question the importance of more and higher education? I was interested even then in what might be described as the profit angle.

• • • • • • • • • • • • • • • • • • • •

I believe I was born

to be an entrepreneur,

as some are born to be

lawyers or left fielders.

• • • • • • • • • • • • • • • • • • • •

Where was the profit angle in school?

This thinking was not necessarily right, nor respectful, but it was not easily shaken. A kid already wary of the conventional order was encouraged to test, or defy, the system.

You are, in fact, reading the words of a high school expellee. Someone who was booted out in his senior year —twice, who received no diploma, no robe, no invitation to the prom.

My father had been dead for nearly two years by that time, so my widowed mother was left to hear the bad news from the school authorities—"rebellious," "fidgety in class," "when he does come to class, given to random mischief." I suppose my infractions were fairly tame by today's standards, but to my high school principal I must have seemed an outlaw.

In junior high I had been president of the student body two years in a row. I had just turned fifteen when my father died, at Christmas, and from then on I developed my instinct for being in trouble. For many, many years I wouldn't celebrate Christmas; a strange, sad gesture for a boy wrestling with becoming a man.

I don't know what made me behave the way I did. There may have been lots of reasons, none very bright, all easy to analyze. My father was a hard working man, a postal inspector, who never drank, never smoked, was never cruel, did most things right. He died at fifty-six. I could probably carry on some about feeling lost and doubting one's values, but that might be putting too fine a point on why and how I reacted as I did.

I'm not sure I was all that complicated. I was spoiled and a natural conniver, the youngest by fifteen years of three brothers. My mother and father were not getting

• • • • • • • • • • • • • • • • • • • •

*I don't take any pride
in saying so, but my
attitude was: If you don't
like me, change my face.
I didn't care much for
people, and I stayed that
way for too many years
to come. It was no one's
fault but my own.
I was always looking for a
shortcut.*

• • • • • • • • • • • • • • • • • • • •

along all that well, and they competed at giving me what-ever I wanted. I played them off against each other, which kids learn to do. I played that game well.

For as long as I could remember, I had saved up to buy that press. In time I hired two other kids to work for me who had been trained in commercial print shops. They were about my age, a real odd couple, a budding young Oscar and Felix. One was neat as a pin, everything immaculate, every job just right. The other was a slob. The slob eventually made money, and the neat one went broke.

We were not very good at what we did, but we were able to put ink on paper. I had success in the neighborhood because most adults would give me an order simply because they couldn't say no to a kid. But I sort of skipped part of my childhood; I kept thinking about business. After I was kicked out of school the second time, I bought a small convenience store. An old Italian gentleman wanted to retire, and I bought the store with a small down pay-ment. I was not yet seventeen.

I kept the store going through most of one winter, but couldn't afford fuel for the stove downstairs. I burned anything I could find to keep the place warm, including some furniture the old man had left in storage. Apparently it was valuable furniture because he was furious when he found out.

Not that his feelings mattered to me. I don't take any pride in saying so, but my attitude was: If you don't like me, change my face. I didn't care much for people, and I stayed that way for too many years to come. It was no one's fault but my own. I was always looking for a shortcut. I learned a valuable lesson from my expulsion. I found out, as few teenagers ever do, exactly who my friends were, and it didn't take long to call roll.

• • • • • • • • • • • • • • • • • • •

There must have been a
fairly complete account of
my misdeeds in there
because the principal was
suitably impressed that I
had amounted to
anything.

• • • • • • • • • • • • • • • • • • •

Right now, no one in America is a bigger believer in education, formal or otherwise, than I. But that came later, with the years and with the process of maturity, something not every teacher or counselor can give you. For what it's worth, I received an honorary degree from my old high school, forty-seven years after I was cashiered. The company I founded, Kwik Kopy, has centers around the world, and our world headquarters in Houston is staffed with people I love. I have no problem telling them so. But getting there was quite a journey.

And, oh yes, there is a sequel and a moral to the tale of my exit from Cranston High. After the rise of Kwik Kopy, a friend of mine took it upon himself to contact the current principal at the school.

The friend, Jan Norris, is a public relations consultant in Houston. He's the kind of fearless character who can pick up a phone, call the White House, and not be surprised when he is put through to the president. Our paths had first crossed when we were on opposite sides in a local political race.

A curious temperament and a good heart prompted Jan to make his call. He asked the principal if he had any record of a student named Bud Hadfield. It didn't take him long to locate the file. There must have been a fairly complete account of my misdeeds in there because the principal was suitably impressed that I had amounted to anything.

Not many weeks later I was standing on the stage at Cranston High in front of a full assembly of the student body receiving a diploma from the school that all those years ago had asked me to leave. You know what? No award, no recognition, has filled me with more satisfaction. I toured the school and felt all manner of emotions— pride, regret, relief, nostalgia, and a longing for those

• •

My belief had been

reaffirmed

that for all things

there is a season.

• •

uncomplicated days of our youth when we had all the answers, never mind the questions.

I noticed they still had the same print shop, the one I had worked in as a student capitalist.

The next day I flew to New York to speak to the Columbia University Graduate School of Business. The date was an unforgettable one, not necessarily related to my appearance. It was October 19, 1987, the day the stock market plunged over five hundred points.

In a question-and-answer period after my speech, one of the future MBA's asked what I thought had caused the crash. "Maybe," I said, "it had a little to do with greed."

I returned to Houston in a philosophical mood. Two weeks later, Jan Norris flew to Rhode Island to deliver a printing press to Cranston High, a gift from its oldest graduate. My belief had been reaffirmed that for all things there is a season.

The year I was seventeen, I caught the travel bug, said "To heck with it," stuck out my thumb and hitchhiked to Hollywood, where one of my brothers was working. I was there a few weeks when I found out that everyone less than eighteen years old had to be in school. So, I turned around and headed back east. I hitched a ride all the way to New York with just enough money to catch a bus from there to Providence.

It was New Year's Eve when I called my mother from Providence. I said, "I'm at the bus station, and I'm coming home."

"All right. So?"

"Well, can you come to Providence and get me?"

"No, I'm busy. If you want to get home, walk."

• • • • • • • • • • • • • • • • • • • •

Success is found
on the other side
of "good enough."

• • • • • • • • • • • • • • • • • • • •

So I walked about four miles to Cranston. When I got there my mother already had a job for me in Vern's Grill as a dishwasher. She figured I needed some humility. My mother was tough, and she had the added advantage of being right.

I lasted a little over a week as a dishwasher. One night I forgot to turn off the fire under the sink and burned the bottom of it. They demoted me to a busboy, picking up dirty dishes. Shortly I fouled up there and was fired.

Without exception, everything I did seemed to turn out wrong. It was soon apparent I was never going to be very good at taking orders from other people. Nor did I appear to have any qualities that recommended me for any special assignments. I was just your basic teenage screwup.

Finally I landed a job that appealed to me, an apprenticeship on the *Washington Post* in the composing room. However, within weeks I had an appendectomy, and while I was recovering at home I heard President Roosevelt on the radio declare that December 7, 1941, would be a date that lived in infamy. The Japanese had bombed Pearl Harbor.

I went to the shipyard in Providence and was hired instantly as a burner—someone who used a blowtorch to burn metal. Then my greetings came from the army. I knew instinctively that I wasn't cut out to be a soldier. I didn't mind the low pay as much as I did the idea of saying "yes, sir" to a lot of people I didn't like or didn't know.

I talked to some of the merchant seamen around the yard who were waiting to take a ship out. I liked what I heard. The money was about three times what any branch of the service paid. The Merchant Marine had reasonably good accommodations, good food and the discipline was

• • • • • • • • • • • • • • • • • • •

Never just do the job.

Put another twelve inches

in your punch.

• • • • • • • • • • • • • • • • • • •

best described as flexible. It was a quasi-military type of service. When you came back from a trip and signed off, you could tell the captain to buzz off if you wanted, and he couldn't do a thing about it…as long as you caught another ship within a certain length of time.

I was accepted by the Merchant Marine Academy, where Benny Leonard, the former world's lightweight boxing champion, was a guest instructor. The first time I saw him he was standing in a circle with a bunch of recruits, just talking. I had no idea who he was. I simply saw a short, skinny runt with a beer belly who must have been in his fifties. He asked if anyone wanted to step in the ring with him, and I let out a chuckle. I was six-foot-two and lanky, but solid. I stepped into the ring and the rest was a blur. He peppered me with punches, lightning fast. From then on I knew who Benny Leonard was. He could have hurt me badly, if he wanted. Instead, he offered advice: "You keep feinting with the left. But when you hit a guy with the right, don't reach for his chin. In your mind, go twelve inches past it and rip his bleeping head off his shoulders."

That lesson served me well in the years ahead. *"Never just do the job. Put another twelve inches in your punch."*

My last bout in the Merchant Marines was with a Texan named Ash. I won the first two rounds, clearly. In the third I was on my toes, dancing, when he nailed me on the chin. I bounced off the mat face first, taking the skin off my forehead. When I came to, I shook my head and said, "I'm ready." Someone said, "You sure are. The fight was over five minutes ago."

In time, I caught my first ship out, the *William S. Cottington*. And in February 1942, I was thrown into that great planetary adventure known as World War II.

• • • • • • • • • • • • • • • • • • • •

Our convoy was four days

out, hugging the coast,

when a British freighter

drifted and rammed us

on the port side.

We knew the ship was

going down, and if we

broke radio silence to send

out an SOS it would tell

the German U-boats the

location of the convoy.

• • • • • • • • • • • • • • • • • • • •

The Providence shipyard turned out Liberty ships, thousands of them, built quickly and cheaply by Henry Kaiser. They were slow, but they held a lot of cargo, and the prevailing wisdom was that one trip across the Atlantic repaid the cost of the ship. If you got blown apart, it was no big loss; they were expendable. The crew tried not to dwell on such implications. Eventually, we learned that our destination was Murmansk, Russia. Our convoy was four days out, hugging the coast, when a British freighter drifted and rammed us on the port side. We knew the ship was going down, and if we broke radio silence to send out an SOS it would tell the German U-boats the location of the convoy. We dropped out and just barely made it into St. John's, Newfoundland. We spent the winter there undergoing repairs.

I was seasick most of the trip. My shipmates used to ask me which side I was on; that's how good a seaman I was. I started out working in the engine room as a fireman, mainly because I had been rejected for radio school and didn't like the three other options—deckhand, purser or working in the galley as a cook. I didn't want to work on deck because it was too cold. So I went down to the engine room, where I worked on the boilers, a job for which I had absolutely no talent. Still, any idiot could do it, and I was no exception.

I took a couple of tests and moved up to other jobs, and gradually settled into a routine. I sailed out of New York. I always had a couple of buddies to hang out with, living high until my money ran out. On one trip, the money went so fast we took part-time jobs at Walgreen's, working the lunch counter. When one of my buddies was on duty, I'd go in and, for a dime, eat three bacon, lettuce and tomato sandwiches. I did the same for them.

• •

I went out and bought a set of records on how to speak French. I played them on a small windup phonograph and kept practicing and practicing. Instead we wound up in Romania.

• •

That was how we fed ourselves.

I will make no attempt here to re-fight the war, other than to say I saw just enough to make me believe that war is vastly overrated as entertainment. I saw people die and corpses floating in the water with no one paying attention; that does something to your soul. It ages you.

In truth, I can't claim that I learned a whole lot at sea other than a little about survival and scavenging. On one trip it was rumored that we were sailing to France. I went out and bought a set of records on how to speak French. I played them on a small windup phonograph and kept practicing and practicing. Instead we wound up in Romania. By the time we made it to France I had learned just enough of the language to do all the ship's negotiating on the black market.

A buddy and I jumped ship in France because we wanted to see Paris. When we came back the ship was gone. We had a frantic time catching up to it. The captain was going to toss us into the brig, but the crew was so shorthanded he couldn't do it.

We did wind up in the brig in Newfoundland, however, under mitigating circumstances. A few of us were caught sneaking beer off an army truck. We felt justified because the army monopolized all the American beer and none was for sale. It wasn't until we raided the truck a second time that they caught us. The ship had to go back to sea, and the captain bailed us out. We pretty much lived a charmed life.

If this sounds like a frivolous way to wage a war, the funny stuff stopped at the water's edge. There were mines and torpedoes and submarines out there. We followed the coastline to resupply the troops and unload tons of

• • • • • • • • • • • • • • • • • •

*I had delivered two dozen
eggs per week to a woman
for an entire year,
and the first time she got
a bad egg she forgot about
all the good ones.
But I took that lesson
to heart. One bad egg can
ruin you. This is politics.
This is business.
This is life.*

• • • • • • • • • • • • • • • • • •

ammunition where historic landings had taken place—
Omaha Beach and Anzio among them. If your ship carried
ammo you earned a bonus, 50 percent more pay, and if
another ship near you went down, you received an additional bonus. Those were hard dollars, and we didn't keep
them long.

There was a certain amount of craziness that I attribute
to being young, halfway around the world, and the need
to prove you weren't frightened. A couple of our crew were
picked up and jailed in Romania—I forget why—just as the
Russians were taking over. I borrowed the captain's coat
and cap, without mentioning it to him. With a buddy, I
went to the jail and bluffed the police into releasing them
just as a Russian contingent was arriving. We ran like hell
back to the ship and that was the last time we went ashore
in that port. It was a dumb thing to do, but not bad training for deals that required quick thinking.

When the war ended in 1945, I had saved nearly
$3,000. I decided to go into the egg business (probably
because I knew nothing about it). I went to the farms,
bought thirty dozen eggs to the carton and took them to
market. I knew how to grade them by scale, but I didn't
know what was called "candling." To "candle" you held a
light up to the egg and whirled it to see if there was anything inside that shouldn't be there.

I had a route in Providence and Cranston and heeded
the advice of one salesman who said, "You don't put your
foot in the door. You put your head in so you can keep
talking." I sold a lot of eggs that first winter. I had to make
my deliveries in a van whose engine rings were shot. Parts
were still unavailable. I had to keep the windows open
because I couldn't see through the smoke that billowed up
from the engine.

• •

There are numerous

opportunities to fail

and generally,

at the moment you fail,

you don't recognize why.

That comes later. It hurts

too much at the moment,

a condition we sometimes

conceal behind jokes.

• •

I gave up on Bud's Fresh Farm Eggs not long after a complaint from my best customer. I had delivered two dozen eggs per week to a woman for an entire year, and the first time she got a bad egg she forgot about all the good ones. But I took that lesson to heart. One bad egg can ruin you. This is politics. This is business. This is life.

In a fairly short period of time, I rang up an impressive record of failed businesses. There was my half-interest in a pig farm; the pigs ate so much I virtually gave my half away. I went broke with an ice cream parlor, a gas station, a frozen food business, a fireworks stand and a personnel agency. Was there a pattern? Yes. In each of them I had no idea what I was doing. I had a whole lot of enthusiasm, but not enough funding.

There are numerous opportunities to fail and generally, at the moment you fail, you don't recognize why. That comes later. It hurts too much at the moment. A pain we sometimes conceal behind jokes. You really want to crawl in a cave and wallow around in your maudlin fit of despair. You think people are looking at you as a loser. When you reflect and analyze it, you say you won't make that mistake again.

Nothing is important unless you do it wrong. Then it becomes paramount.

At some point, I had a job in an amusement park, went through a first marriage, and wound up setting type at the *Berkshire Courier* in Great Barrington, Massachusetts. One morning I stepped outside. It was twenty degrees below zero and my car wouldn't start. I had to walk to work. I decided then this was not how I wanted to begin my days.

By then my brother Ben had moved from California and was living in Houston. I called and asked him if he

BUD'S BUSINESS DOZEN #1

Trust
your
intuition.

thought I could find a job there. Ben said, "Things are so good down here even you can get a job."

I was encouraged by his optimism.

I was twenty-four years old and about to start a new life in a city two thousand miles away. I could barely locate it on a map. I borrowed my mother's car, hitched a sixteen-foot house trailer to it and rolled into Houston on a Sunday. I found a job on Monday and went to work on Tuesday. A few months later, I spotted an ad in the paper for the Wickman Printing Company. It was located at Whitney and Yale streets in a building eighteen by twenty feet. It was owned by a woman whose husband ran the print shop. She wanted a thousand dollars for the shop and its inventory and would rent the building for $20 a month.

My brother and I each put up $250, and she agreed to carry the other $500. When my brother brought in a friend of his named Smith, we changed the name from Wickman Printing to Smith and Hadfield.

We worked out of that location for the next two or three years with no running water. We had to use a restroom at a Texaco station a good mile down the road. The landlady gave me a bucket of water to wash my hands each day. The first addition we built was a bathroom with a stand-up shower. It was so tight we had to use the shower curtain for a door. Actually, we couldn't afford a door. That is how we started out in the printing business.

Our next move was to West Crosstimbers, where we put up an L-shaped building and added office supplies to the print shop. One day Ben, who I always believed was smarter than I, said he and Smith wanted to do away with the printing. All I had was a third of the vote, so I suggested we strike some kind of deal. "Figure out what each part is

●●●●●●●●●●●●●●●●●●●●●

Partners are permissible,
but the "golden rule"
is this:
The guy with 51 percent
of the stock
makes the rules.

●●●●●●●●●●●●●●●●●●●●●

worth," I said, "and let me buy out the printing."

They obviously wanted to keep the building, so I asked them to set a price and give me a thirty-day option.

I went down to a savings and loan and had no trouble borrowing enough money to pay for the building in full. I also had enough left over to provide working capital for the print shop. As I figured, the building was worth several thousand more than they projected.

I paid off and rented half the building to them and that covered my payment to the bank. We actually partitioned the building, and I kept the print shop. I didn't do badly on that deal.

Among the lessons I learned was to avoid having partners. I never recommend it. Partners are permissible, but the "golden rule" is this: The guy with 51 percent of the stock makes the rules. One person must be responsible for the bottom line. Someone has to have control, someone has to be subservient.

When you start out as partners, you wind up as enemies. Dissension happens when the honeymoon ends.

I learned not to take a minority position in a company. I will not take an active position in anyone else's company. The bottom line responsibility and the bottom line say-so are what interest me.

Twice, before I found my niche, I tried to go into the franchise business—in picture framing and photo finishing. When people tell me there is a lot of money in picture framing, I reply, "Yes, and $300,000 of it is mine." That was what I lost. I lacked the expertise, and the lesson still hadn't sunk in. Then I went into photo finishing. I had a great idea: to put together a photo lab where the customers came in with a roll of film and a clerk showed them how to put it in the

● ● ● ● ● ● ● ● ● ● ● ● ● ● ● ● ● ● ● ●

*Babe Ruth was the
greatest home run hitter
of his time, and the
records he established
lasted fifty years. He hit
714 homers, but he struck
out 1,330 times.*

● ● ● ● ● ● ● ● ● ● ● ● ● ● ● ● ● ● ● ●

machine, how to run it through the developer, how to turn it...the whole process. I even conducted free classes on photography. The customers said, "We'll pay you extra to run the film through for us." And I said, "No, that's not consistent with our policy." A year or so later, a company came along that called itself Fotomat and made a few million dollars. You have seen them all over the world.

The lesson is: LISTEN TO YOUR CUSTOMERS. Really listen! We do. We listen to our franchise owners because they are in the trenches. If they say, "I don't think this will work," I need to know why. They generally have a good reason. You simply can't stand off at a distance and direct a fight. You have to be in the ring, or at least in the corner.

I'm not afraid of failing. Thomas Edison claimed to have made fifty thousand attempts to build a storage battery. When he was asked if he ever intended to give up, he said, "No. I now know fifty thousand things that won't work."

Then there was a merchant who owned a little country store and went broke in '31. He failed as a lawyer. Was inducted into the army as a captain, sent west to fight the Indians and came home demoted to private. He was defeated for the legislature in '32. He again failed in business in '34, He had a nervous breakdown in '36. He lost another election in '38, was defeated for Congress in '46 and again in '48. He was defeated for vice-president in '56 and the Senate in '58. He was elected President in 1860 and he signed every document. His name was Abe Lincoln.

Babe Ruth was the greatest home run hitter of his time, and the records he established lasted fifty years. He hit 714 homers, but he struck out 1,330 times.

Failure is not in losing,

but in giving up

the idea that

winning is

no longer worthwhile.

They all understood something that most people will never get through their thick heads. Failing is part of the learning process. Failure is not in losing, but in giving up the idea that winning is no longer worthwhile.

By 1966, I guess we had flat run out of reasons to fail. At last, we knew them all. That year I started a company called Instant Print. I knew we were into the big time because I got a letter from a lawyer in Chicago. The letter said if we continued to use that name, they would sue us, throw us in jail, take away our children—the usual threats.

I told my wife, Mary, "I've blown it again, it's all over. We can't use Instant Print anymore—a great name." Mary said, "Well, why don't you give it a new name? Call it Quick Copy with a K."

I said, "That's hokey."

She said, "You could have one K chasing another K."

I said, "That sounds like something you'd see on a hardware store in Deckers Prairie. Nobody will buy it." Still, I called a friend of mine, an illustrator at the *Houston Post*, Dick Putney. I said, "Dick, Mary has an idea. She wants to make a logo—I'm a little embarrassed to tell you..." I explained it to him. I said don't spend too much time. Do it while you watch the football game...keep the price down.

That afternoon, Dick gave me the logo and it had one K chasing another K, Kwik Kopy. We have never changed it to this day. He charged me $7.50, and I have to say it has been the best return on any of my investments.

Chapter

2

What,
Me Worry?

• •

Minute for minute and dollar for dollar, the Dale Carnegie course was the best investment I ever made. There would not be a Kwik Kopy today without the self-improvements I was able to make.

• •

It is hard, if not impossible, to develop an effective management style when you tend to spend much of your time arguing with your customers, or on occasion engaging them in fist fights. This was one of my problems when I was persuaded thirty-odd years ago to take the Dale Carnegie course.

I am not going to repeat the Carnegie principles here. What matters is that I began to change, to adjust, to respond. At the time of my first class I didn't own a suit or a necktie. I went with an attitude that bordered on belligerent. I made it clear that I felt under duress. It took five or six sessions before I understood what they were trying to do.

I didn't fully understand what the course really was until years later. It is not just a course in public speaking or in human relations (in a university they would probably call it Humanities I, II and III). It covers the complex dynamics of how man relates to man and his environment.

Minute for minute and dollar for dollar, the Dale Carnegie course was the best investment I ever made. There would not be a Kwik Kopy today without the self-improvements I was able to make. I truly believe this, and

• • • • • • • • • • • • • • • • • •

The last perfect man
walked on this planet two
thousand years ago. Yet
too many people expect
themselves to achieve this
kind of grade.

• • • • • • • • • • • • • • • • • •

I don't own a single share of Dale Carnegie stock.

The Dale Carnegie course gave me the courage to really analyze myself. There are many things I am aware of, when I do them, that I know are not necessarily right or prudent. I still have a short wick and a bad temper, but at least when I lose my cool, I know it. I don't expect self-perfection. The last perfect man walked on this planet two thousand years ago. Yet too many people expect to achieve that kind of grade. When they fall short, there is the danger they will quit altogether. It's like going on a diet. A person eats a candy bar and says, "Oh, to heck with the diet. I've blown it now." So he or she eats everything in sight.

We do the same thing mentally. "Gee, I didn't get the promotion so I'm giving up the job, or getting out of the business." Or: "I estimated the job wrong. I guess that means I don't know how to do an estimate. I can't make it in this business." Negative thoughts, like mushrooms, grow in the dark and dampness.

A little background might be helpful here. I finally gave in and went to the Dale Carnegie course at the persistent urging of Ro Croes—the full name is Rosimbo Croes. He's from Aruba. We met when he was a bookkeeper in a lumberyard that became a customer of mine. I sold him an adding machine. We argued about the price, as we argued about most things. We became good friends, and he invested in the company that preceded Kwik Kopy, along with a partner, a woman who became a real horse's behind.

One day she was at the center, screaming at Ro, "I want to sell my stock in this lousy company." He said, "How much do you want for your stock?" She said, "All I want is my money back." She had invested $7,000. He said, "Fine, bring the stock by tonight, and I'll have a check ready."

• •

Negative thoughts,
like mushrooms, grow in the
dark and dampness.

• •

She reappeared later that night with her husband and her attorney and an escalated price. Ro patiently repeated, "I'll give you $7,000 and not one penny more." This went on for a couple of hours.

She and her escorts walked out in anger. Half an hour later, her husband returned, threw the stock on the counter and said, "Give me the check." When he was gone, I said, "Ro, you're the greatest negotiator I've ever seen." He replied, "Bud, that was no negotiation. That was all the money I have, every cent."

He is an astute businessman who taught me to be attentive. We would have mini-board meetings of the company, which was known then as Bud Hadfield Printers. Whenever I wanted to spend money, he made me justify it. I reached a point where I almost disliked him, but he was 100 percent right. Now, I make others justify their spending in the same way. In the early 1960s Ro and I were the board of directors. He worried about me, especially my quick temper.

Ro was in the office the day I got into a fight with Bob Horowitz, actually a friend of mine who owned Big Boy Tool Company. The clash began as one of those "one up on you" games where you rap one another on the arm, until one guy hit too hard and it escalated from there. It blew up into a full-scale brawl, with chairs and tables knocked over, papers scattered, and blood on the floor. When we washed up I discovered that the blood was mine, which is the very worst kind. I clearly came out second best, which in those days was not uncommon.

Ro was visibly disturbed. One day he came by and said, "Bud, why don't you take the Dale Carnegie course? I think it could help you." I said no, as far as I was concerned it was Mickey Mouse.

• •

It took me a long time to
realize that
you have no right to
impose your company
above another person's
consideration of their
family. The biggest
mistake I made was
sacrificing so much of my
own family life
for Kwik Kopy.

• •

He was taking the course at the time and excited about it. He kept bringing it up and finally he bargained: "If you'll take the course, I'll go with you. I'll even pick you up and bring you home." I agreed. The company would pay the enrollment fee. I knew nothing about Carnegie or the program. I thought it was basically a charm school. Soon I realized it was the most misunderstood course in America.

I was working eighteen hours a day then, seven days a week. I confused activity with achievement. I learned at Carnegie that you earn the right to talk about those things you have lived through or thoroughly studied. You don't go off into ethereal toots. I have no time for the problematical discussion. I want facts. I want flesh-and-blood situations.

It took me a long time to realize that you have no right to impose your company above another person's consideration for their family. The biggest mistake I made was sacrificing much of my own family life for Kwik Kopy. I should have been paying attention to them.

I remember the day Mary plopped our young son Jimmy on my lap and said, "Talk to him."

"What about?"

"Anything," she said. "You haven't seen him in a week."

I met Mary at Dale Carnegie in 1958. By then I was an instructor, having plunged into it as I did most things— obsessively. Naturally, she took an immediate dislike to me. This is how Mary tells the story:

"I went to what they call a Dale Carnegie demonstration session at the Rice Hotel, with about sixty people on hand. After the session was over we went outside the

• •

Hokey works. I love it.
That's why people go to
Disney World.
—Mary Hadfield

• •

ballroom and sat across the table from a salesman where Bud was helping sell the course. He was not my instructor that night, but I remember sitting across the table from him, thinking I didn't like him worth a hoot. I thought, 'This guy is as phony as a three-dollar bill.' He was very gregarious.

"I was only half-serious about being there. But, I felt I really needed the course. In later years, it was fun to watch people stand up and tell why they wanted to take the Dale Carnegie course. Ninety-nine times out of a hundred they are there to gain self-confidence. I knew that was why I was there and I said so. But most people won't admit this. They say, 'I came so I will remember names,' or 'my boss made me,' or 'I'm going to be speaking to this big group and I need a quick brush-up.' By the end of the course they are secure enough to admit the truth.

"I don't know what it was about Bud. I bought the course, so he must have been a good salesman. Later on, he instructed part of my sessions. I found he was very genuine. It's not the Carnegie formula so much that people initially resist, it's just that people often look at something and say, that's hokey. Let me tell you something. Hokey works. I love it. That's why people go to Disney World."

Meeting Mary was another turning point in my life and in the development of Kwik Kopy. She has her own ideas and convictions. She questions, argues, challenges your thinking. The half-modern, half-rustic campus that houses the Kwik Kopy family in northwest Houston is in large part a product of her taste and imagination.

I can't claim that Carnegie endowed me with patience, but I developed more than I had. It also turned out to be a very effective source of networking, and among unlikely characters.

BUD'S BUSINESS DOZEN　　　　　**#2**

ALWAYS REMEMBER

No one is unimportant.

Hal Husbands was the warden at the Texas men's penitentiary in Sugar Land, known as Central Number One. I suppose there may still be people out there who wouldn't know Dale Carnegie from the Carnegie deli in New York. Hal wasn't one of them.

The Texas Department of Corrections was the first in the country to offer a Carnegie program, and all the books and supplies were furnished at no cost by Dale Carnegie Institute. The instructors also dedicated their time at no cost. Hal was a vigorous supporter. He had read Dale Carnegie's renowned *How to Win Friends and Influence People* and was impressed with Carnegie's principles. Hal was constantly searching for something to help reform prisoners. His philosophy was if he helped just one man, it would be worth the trouble.

The Carnegie sponsor in Houston was Jim Trivette, a fine man who made the commitment on behalf of Carnegie to Hal and the men of Central Number One. Hal takes great pride in knowing that not just one life changed, but many inmates were transformed into productive, law-abiding citizens because of his decision to give the course a try.

The friendship between Hal Husbands and myself grew. We developed a close relationship based on mutual respect. Hal felt Dale Carnegie techniques showed a man's true nature. If he was a hardened con man then this would win out. But, if a man truly wanted to change, Carnegie could help him achieve this.

Here is one of Hal's favorite success stories:

"The general manager of the Texas prison system wanted to see the final session of one of the classes. There were usually around sixty people in attendance. We invited about forty inmates, and the families and friends of those

• • • • • • • • • • • • • • • • • •

*Pressure is when you
have people you
like betting on
you to win.*

• • • • • • • • • • • • • • • • • •

speaking, as well as officials. In this class I had one man whom I picked because he was shy. I tried to pick out every kind of personality I could think of for the classes. This particular man was so bashful that he couldn't even look you in the eye. He would drop his eyes when he passed you in the hall. In the first session all you have to do is state your name and where you are from. He couldn't get up and say his name. In the final speech you have to tell the audience why you took the course and what you learned from it. When this man made his final speech, he stood up and scanned the audience, making eye contact as he said, 'I took the course because the warden wanted me to (they're taught to tell the truth), and what I got out of it is, I feel like a man who has walked out of a dark cave.' Here was a man who was beat and struggling with an inferiority complex of tremendous weight, yet he had the courage to begin again. That really made an impression on me."

I will never forget the day that Hal showed me a steel file that was shaved into a point so fine it looked like a long toothpick. "Where did you get this?" I asked. "Took it out of a dead Mexican's back," he replied. It was a different world behind "The Walls," and Husbands knew that world better than anyone I ever met. He also knew that one individual could make a difference.

I picked the members of Kwik Kopy's board of directors because I trusted them as friends. I didn't tell them to buy stock so I could put them on the board. I figured that they had invested in me and they deserved a place on the board.

Jimmy Patterson was another Carnegie instructor, the president of a small, successful company. Henry Eason was someone I've known almost from the day I moved to Houston. Calvin Finley worked for the city. Jim Mills was

• • • • • • • • • • • • • • • • • • •

I would rather go to a loan shark than to the public money market.

• • • • • • • • • • • • • • • • • • •

a vice president of McKesson-Robbins, a man of highly re-
fined business instincts. When you start franchising, you
always have a cash flow problem, a need for money on a
continuing basis. All of them bought stock and got their
friends to do the same.

Others were there at the start. Joe Lill was one of my
first owners. Calvin Finley took every dime he had out of
the bank to invest in Kwik Kopy. As did Ro Croes. Pressure is when you have people you like betting on you to
win. There really wasn't much selling. The usual conversation consisted of my saying, "I'm starting a new business,
and I'm looking for investors. Want to do it?" "Sure." "You
want to know about it?" "No."

I'm pleased to say they have been rewarded many
times over.

Of course, everyone understood that we would not
take the company public. This position is the heart of our
philosophy. One of my friendly competitors, Bill LeVine,
and I went separate ways when he did go public. That isn't
to say I was right and he was wrong. There are two reasons to go public: (1) to raise money, or (2) to get your
money out of the business. I made a trade-off. I would
rather go to a loan shark than to the public money market
simply because I don't want my business subject to any
more government and other outside intrusion than absolutely necessary.

In my experience most officers of a public company are
more interested in the quarterly statement than the success
of the business. This is how they keep their jobs. Europeans
and Asians don't think that way. They're looking years
down the road. A builder in Houston's Galleria-area told
me he had to be thinking five years ahead.

• •

You don't go bear hunting

with a B-B gun.

• •

At Kwik Kopy we try to do our planning a year in advance. Our budget for next year has to be within a point or two of being right on the button. A slight deviation can knock me out of the buggy in terms of where the company is going. You don't go bear hunting with a B-B gun. You have to be prepared to deal with the unexpected.

Every week, our chief financial officer tells me what is in the bank, what we owe, and what's coming in. Even on weekends, we transfer money. Your money has to work for you twenty-four hours a day. A fellow who hasn't been in business before looks in the cash register and thinks, "That's all mine." But it isn't. It belongs to the vendors, to his employees, to debt retirement, to interest, to royalties.

The chief executive officer of any company has to be a generalist. An accountant thinks in terms of accounting. A lawyer thinks in terms of law. A CEO must think in complete terms. This is why experience is beyond price. It is a whispering voice that reminds us of our past mistakes.

In the early years, our biggest problem was generating enough capital to allow us to grow. We were constantly fighting to make the next payroll. Later we made three physical moves in about six years because of rapid growth.

Those were exciting and often scary times. By 1970, we were standing at the threshold of a new printing technology. We were in on the ground floor and rolled pretty high in a robust economy. I've always had targets. I am totally goal oriented. Our budgets were not as professional as they probably needed to be, but we were flying by the seat of our pants. When you are in a period of rapid expansion, you are working without a net. The potential is there for as many mistakes as advances.

Expertise in the industry had not developed. It still

• •

In a life-or-death situation,
you throw pride
out the window.

• •

wasn't that complex. I was hiring experienced printers and accountants. We had a high turnover rate because of my short fuse. During this growth, we had no in-house training to help our employees improve.

In a sense, we have spent over twenty-five years putting our training program together. I came into this business with ideas and through the years developed an expertise in management. I learned to read a financial statement. I also learned early that if I couldn't do this someone would take the company. I'm not bashful about asking questions. I wear out my lawyers and accountants, asking "Why, why, why? Tell me again." In a life-or-death situation, you throw pride out the window.

Kwik Kopy was born during a collision of the old and the new. In the first few years there were a few changes in technology; not the way it is today. Computers and electronic typesetting were on the horizon. When we started, we had one tiny sliver in the spectrum of graphics, and over the years our share has broadened. It used to be black on white, then we advanced to colors and moved on. We kept the concept that we always printed it quickly; we couldn't fall into the trap of being what was called a job shop, which is almost extinct. We do what they used to do, but we do it a lot faster for less money and, in most cases, better quality.

A few years ago, I felt a poignant tug when I made a trip to Boston and met a man named Lyons who still ran an old letter press shop. He had the most complete collection of wood and metal type in America. At that point, he was right at one hundred years old. They had one old-time, automatic press, and I asked one of his workers how long they had had the Kluge. He said, "That's the new one. We bought it back in the '40s."

• • • • • • • • • • • • • • • • • • • •

On the plains of
hesitation, bleach the
bones of countless
millions who,
on the threshold of
victory, sat down to wait
and in waiting, died.
—William Moulton Marshton

• • • • • • • • • • • • • • • • • • • •

He hadn't changed anything. One of our vendors had bought the rights to his type, which is also a hobby of mine. I consider myself a compositor, and he had some very old esoteric type faces. We drove Mr. Lyons home, and on the way he said, in a quavery and slightly scolding voice, "Mr. Hadfield, aren't you ashamed of what you did to the small printers around the country?"

I didn't know how to answer him. Believe me, I felt his pain. Truth was, just as horses gave way to trains and trains to planes, the change had to happen. He was right. In the printing industry, I was part of making it happen.

But this was and is the mind-set of many printers. Put your head in the sand, don't make changes, and things will turn out all right. I fear complacency and strive to keep our heads out of the sand. We have to keep up with new technology, even if it is too unproven to use. We can't wait to hear about it from our franchise owners.

Mr. Lyons died a year or two after our visit. He was a gallant gentleman. I did finally give him an answer, but it was lame. I told him I had been a letterpress printer most of my life and I had simply recognized that change was inevitable. Ten years from now, someone will talk in the same generalities about today's technology. They will wake and discover that the self-imaging camera is no longer the latest thing.

William Moulton Marshton put it this way: "On the plains of hesitation bleach the bones of countless millions who, on the threshold of victory, sat down to wait and in waiting, died."

Chapter

3
The Franchise

••••••••••••••••••••

What we call "philosophy"

is simply the sum

of what we have learned

from all the experiences life

has thrown at us,

the good, the bad

and the in-between.

••••••••••••••••••••

W hat we call "philosophy" is simply the sum of what we have learned from all the experiences life has thrown at us, the good, the bad and the in-between.

Kwik Kopy's philosophy is everywhere you walk, everywhere you turn on the campus we built on the fringes of big, bustling Houston, in the woods near Cypress, Texas. It is in wooden signs hammered into the ground that say in blue letters: "Tomorrow Belongs to Kwik Kopy." "Earn the Right to Be Proud." I believe in slogans. And I believe in people. Our most valuable inventory goes home every night.

When you interview a job applicant, nine out of ten will tell you they are a "people person." Not all of them are. You have to listen to what they say and how they express what they feel. I believe I qualify as one now, but it took quite a while and a serious re-tooling.

Among the more valuable lessons I have learned is to give my top people their space, give them enough air. If they are going to be decent leaders, they can't be puppets. Our managers all do things I disapprove of, but they need that latitude. Keeping your mouth closed isn't always easy, but I'm working on it.

● ● ● ● ● ● ● ● ● ● ● ● ● ● ● ● ● ● ●

To start a business and to
run it successfully,
you have to like people.
You have to care
about them.

● ● ● ● ● ● ● ● ● ● ● ● ● ● ● ● ● ● ●

Some of our managers have literally grown up before my eyes—Steve Hammerstein, Perry Hillegeist, Harish Babla, Pattie Paddy, Brian Gay, among others. I will offer my best input as forcefully as I can, but if they choose to go another way, who is to say I'm right?

Once, I purchased a large offset press, the biggest press I ever owned. We had to use a crane to set it up. When it was finally in place, the foreman of our printing department came out, walked all the way around it, and said, "I never saw a Harris press that worked worth a darn." Three months later they hauled it off. Dale Carnegie said, "Let the other man feel the idea is his." If you want to develop a leader, you don't try to jam your ideas down his or her throat.

To start a business and to run it successfully, you have to like people. You have to care about them. And you have to know how to hire and fire them.

Firing someone is the meanest part of anyone's job. I compare it to a dentist pulling a tooth. You don't dawdle, you don't make them suffer, you get it over with fast. This isn't anyone's idea of fun. It is a cold reality of today's business culture. I have developed my own procedure. I first go to the personnel department and ask if there is anything else I need to know. You have to be sure you are right. If I am, I do it. I don't change my mind. I hand the person an envelope. Inside is a letter of resignation. A check for a month's salary is waiting for them in the accounting office. We tell them we had the wrong job for them, and they can do better somewhere else. If anyone calls for a job reference, this is the information we pass along.

It may be a failure not just on his part, but ours, too. Every time you fire someone, a part of the history of your

• • • • • • • • • • • • • • • • • • •

I come down on our
people hard, because I
want them to improve.
I want them to succeed.
When I chew someone
out, it takes an average of
fifteen to twenty seconds.
I don't cook them over a
slow grill. I throw them in
the microwave.

• • • • • • • • • • • • • • • • • • •

company walks out the door with them. And you don't get it back.

The task is distasteful, and I don't pass it down the line. In our company I fire the officers, if necessary, and that is no pleasure trip. I had to fire a chief financial officer a few years ago. His reports were not accurate and that, in my book, is tantamount to lying. If I couldn't rely on his reports, I could not rely on him.

The situation you dread is when a good person does a poor job. Bum Phillips, the former football coach, said there were two kinds of players to avoid: the ones who won't do what you tell them, and the ones who won't do anything except what you tell them. Our version of that individual is the employee who is not good enough to promote and too good to fire.

My rules are about as basic as the Ten Commandments. If someone lies to me, or steals from me, he's gone. If he makes the same mistake over and over, he's gone. I treat the people who work in grounds maintenance and in the cafeteria better than the ones in the office. I am not a "do-gooder," but if I don't stick up for them, who will? No one in your organization should be made to feel that in the order of priority, they rate just below the person who feeds the goldfish.

I believe in striking a balance. You need discipline, and compassion. I want things done now, and I don't want to explain myself twice. But if an employee comes to me and he's hurting and needs a thousand dollars, I usually give it to him and don't ask why.

I come down on our people hard, because I want them to improve. I want them to succeed. When I chew someone out, it takes an average of fifteen to twenty seconds. I

• • • • • • • • • • • • • • • • • • • •

*At Kwik Kopy we never
hesitate to hire a young
person with little or
no experience.*

• • • • • • • • • • • • • • • • • • • •

don't cook them over a slow grill. I throw them in the microwave. They don't have to go back to their desk and wonder if I'm unhappy or not. When you give them a chewing out, what you are doing is telling them you want them to make it. If you fire them, they're gone. If you bawl them out, you live with them later.

I don't go ballistic on someone who tries but screws up. I had an employee make a mistake that cost us $52,000 on a deal. I said, "Mike, you screwed up."

"Yes, sir."

"You really feel bad about it?"

"Yes, sir. I want to die right now."

"Do me a favor, Mike. I hold the record around here for the biggest screw up. Quit trying to break it. Now get back to work." You don't vent your anger over an honest mistake that anyone might have made.

Once, I chewed out a vice president, unaware that the sound of my voice was carrying through the air conditioning vent in my office and out near the elevator. Some of our employees had their vocabulary enriched that day, not at all to my credit. Every now and then I chew out the entire company in an employee meeting. On one occasion, they had become sloppy around the building. I told them, "You're like pigs. You throw cigarettes in the urinals. Would you do that at home?"

In the last three years I haven't been able to come up with a really valid reason for a group flogging. The fact is, I really love them.

At Kwik Kopy we never hesitate to hire a young person with little or no experience. For example, a fire chief's son came to me for a job. His only skill was he could fly a plane. We didn't have an opening or a plane. But that

● ●

God brings you good

people at His convenience,

not when you need them.

● ●

wasn't important. He had been a student at Texas A&M, where they teach discipline. He was all "yes, sir," and "no, sir." I'll take a fresh, bright young mind over an old hard head any time. They don't have any bad habits or stale ideas to unlearn.

Besides, God brings you good people at His convenience, not when you need them. We put them in training, and then the word gets around that he or she has potential, and the different departments compete for them. This makes me fairly popular until I make the decision.

I rarely get involved in the interviewing process. The department heads will haul them in to gauge their compatibility. I stick my head in to ask one or two questions, never about the job. One employee says that during her interview, all I asked was if she played tennis.

Our rule of thumb is that if they last a year, they generally stay. Bob Harrison has been with us fourteen years, Steve Hammerstein ten. Henry Eason has been with us almost from the beginning, even though I fired him once. He wasn't with the company when he had a heart attack in New Orleans. As they were wheeling him into the hospital, he said, "If I die, I want Bud Hadfield to handle my estate. I don't like the S.O.B., but he's honest."

Maurine Hulsey, who headed up our Demand Graphics Research department, is typical of our hiring practices. She had her own company, which specialized in records management. Our records were a mess, and we hired her on a fee basis to straighten them out. When she was almost finished, I asked, "What happens after you leave?"

She said, "What do you mean?"

"What kind of condition will these records be in a year from now?" I asked.

• • • • • • • • • • • • • • • • • • •

Fear of failure is my
body guard.
It keeps my ego in check.

• • • • • • • • • • • • • • • • • • •

"If you're like most companies," she replied, "in a year they'll be a mess again."

So I convinced her to come to work for us, and today we depend on Maurine for a list of things too long to itemize.

This background is essential to understanding how we operate at Kwik Kopy, how we conduct our classes and train our franchise owners. And how each relates to the other. Fear of failure is my bodyguard. It keeps my ego in check.

In 1967, we founded the company that became Kwik Kopy, and at virtually the same time decided to go into franchising. There was an industry already out there, but the problem was that no regulations existed. There were no standards and no real precedents in the field of instant printing. I fight and oppose government regulations more than most, but in any business you need a semblance of order.

I remember going to a franchise show where a fellow had a booth promoting a fast food chain. He had a young couple standing at a cash register, calling out to the visitors, "All you do is fill up this cash register all day long." People were believing it. I wanted to throw up.

Many franchising companies started in California, which may not surprise you. California was the first of seventeen states to adopt regulations to govern the industry. We joined the leading trade association, and one or more of us attended the seminars that were offered. We met a lot of charlatans. This was a whole new Garden of Eden. One fellow contacted me and said, "We'll sell your franchises for you and relieve you of that responsibility."

I asked what the terms were.

• • • • • • • • • • • • • • • • • • • •

An entrepreneur will try

to be different even if it

costs more.

• • • • • • • • • • • • • • • • • • • •

"You pay me $5,000 for each client I bring in. We can probably get you fifty a year."

I said, "I can't train fifty a year."

He said, "So? What do you care?"

In today's environment, no one goes into it feeling that they are joining the circus. We tell our prospects to consult their lawyers, bankers and accountants, all of whom are usually negative. We want them to have all the negative feedback they can tolerate. If they want answers, we quote the old Packard slogan—ask the man who owns one. A list of all our franchise owners, names and phone numbers, is part of our disclosure. The owners are free to tell them whatever they want; we have no control over the information they exchange.

I gave that advice once to a man from Virginia, and he replied, "I've already talked to twenty of your owners." I asked him, out of honest curiosity, what they told him. "I didn't hear a negative word," he said. "But they all said you have to work hard, real hard."

No one who acquires a Kwik Kopy center is investing in a job. If they think it will take the same effort and energy as a job with a large corporation, then they shouldn't get into it. The first few years are not just tough, they can be miserable.

An entrepreneur is not necessarily the ideal candidate, either. He can be a problem because he reacts in a totally different manner. An entrepreneur will try to be different even if it costs more. With Kwik Kopy our franchisees buy a system. They need to use it if they want their money's worth.

As we went along in the early years, we sort of wrote our own book on franchising. Although franchising in

• • • • • • • • • • • • • • • • • • •

I always observe the
principle recommended by
Henry Ford, who always
hired people smarter
than he was.

• • • • • • • • • • • • • • • • • • •

many areas is poorly regarded as a way of doing business, I don't know if I would change much of what we have done.

I had a woman in my office one day who wanted to franchise her temporary help agency. She had spent $100,000 with one consulting firm, and all they had sent her were poorly done boilerplate contracts. She received absolutely no value for her money.

I told her, "You've already dropped a hundred thousand down the drain. If you want to get into franchising, the best way to go is to hire someone with extensive experience. It doesn't have to be a lawyer. They will tell you what kind of professional help is needed. This is not a do-it-yourself project."

I always observe the principle recommended by Henry Ford, who always hired people smarter than he was. Once, he was being examined by a high-powered lawyer representing the other side in a suit. The lawyer asked a series of unusual questions, aimed at establishing that Mr. Ford was not too bright. Finally, Ford said, "I have a panel of buttons on this desk. If I need to know answers to your silly questions, all I have to do is press one of these buttons."

There are no buttons in the franchise business today, no way to know all the answers. It requires a team effort. The Kwik Kopy campus is testimony to our belief in that concept.

It has been described as a "corporate amusement park," a description that doesn't offend us. The grounds are pastoral. Ducks swim in a man-made lake. There are western-style log cabins with dozens of private rooms for guests and a full-size replica of the Alamo. A wooden stock-

• • • • • • • • • • • • • • • • • • • •

People are really
wonderful. Some never
learn to accept it.

• • • • • • • • • • • • • • • • • • • •

ade conceals a bank of air conditioners, and the cafeteria is in a log cabin.

Initially, we ran into some resistance to our plans to re-create the Alamo. The Daughters of the Republic of Texas refused to share the blueprints of the Texas shrine. So I sent some of our employees on a holiday with their children and told them to take hundreds of pictures of the Alamo. When ours was completed, with stone quarried in Mexico, there were no more objections. The replica is not a tourist attraction. It was built faithfully and with respect. People tend to whisper when they walk through it.

Mary did the interior designs for both the Inn and the Alamo. Her job title is vice president of education, but her touch is everywhere. She has a lovely, Jessica Tandy quality about her, gentle with a no-nonsense streak. I've known few people who were more versatile. Mary gave Kwik Kopy its name. She taught classes in typesetting and published our magazine for years. I tease her about being soft on her staff, and she accuses me of being too hard on mine.

Central to our success is the mandatory training program, which brings in new franchise owners from locations around the globe. They take one look at the tranquil grounds, the swimming pool and tennis court and think they have signed on with Club Med. They are quickly disabused of any ideas that their stay will constitute a vacation.

They are in for a dawn-to-dusk grind, making their way not much after sunrise from the log cabins to the Alamo, where classes—consisting of up to fourteen students—start at 7 a.m. The course takes three weeks, and we expect them to be punctual. One group of students came in late to find their instructor going ahead without them, talking to an empty room. They asked what he was

In Pursuit of Excellence

One day an eagle will fly higher than any eagle has ever flown before. The sky is a living, ever-present challenge the eagle will never conquer, nor will the sky ever tame the will of the eagle.

This endless pursuit, beyond any reach, could be perceived by the eagle as the pursuit of excellence.

Life is a pursuit—a journey to excellence. A journey without final destination.

It is a continuing desire to hold on for reason to live—one more year—one more month—one more week—one more day—one more minute.

For life is excellence and the pursuit of excellence is life.

And I live.

Thank you, God.

— Bud Hadfield

doing. "Holding class," he said. "What are you doing?"

We have no illusions about how much education we can cram into their brains. We take someone, for example, who has been wearing green eyeshades for twenty years and train him to run a business in three weeks. It's enough to make the gods laugh.

Anita Bonser, the training director, and her staff adjust and fine-tune the program almost weekly. The company used to lodge our students in a nearby motel, but that only exposed them to taverns and other local distractions. Now we isolate them.

Some of the teaching is fundamental: pricing, job scheduling, inventory. The focus in the training is management skills and selling but, above all, confidence building.

A lawyer once said to me, "You know, you're not too bright." I asked him to be more specific. "To run a franchise company," he said, "you need to lease the space and rent the office equipment in case you have to move on in a hurry."

We do exactly the opposite. We put down roots. Roots don't pull you back, they hold you up like a tree. Our centers are on a lease-purchase agreement. Like many of the old European immigrants, I have to own the land. In Italy, the farmer buys a couple of acres and uses every inch of it. That is a fine feeling. We elected to build our own facilities, and our campus can accommodate over ninety people overnight in the three inns, including the Alamo and the log cabins plus our recently completed La Hacienda. In this environment, we can nurture the relationship with the new franchise owners.

Without sounding patronizing, the early stages are not unlike a parent-child relationship. The child reaches for your hand as you cross the street. Later they want to walk

BUD'S BUSINESS DOZEN   **#3**

If you wouldn't
buy it,
then don't
sell it.

ahead and do it on their own, acting as if they don't know you. The relationship matures or it falls apart. Generally, it matures.

Most instructors are home grown and we draw from the corporate staff. Even our officers teach. I'm not aware of many companies where this is done. A reporter for *The Wall Street Journal* expressed amazement upon seeing our employee loyalty in action: "They police the grounds without pay," he wrote. "They work weekends without pay. They fill the parking lot at 7:30 a.m. for jobs that begin at 8."

By the end of 1990 we had tightened our position as the second largest company in the instant printing field— we are now the largest. We held our most successful annual conference in Houston, with former President Ronald Reagan and Dr. Norman Vincent Peale as speakers. Internationally, Kwik Kopy was now represented in Canada, England, Australia, Israel, South Africa, Mexico, Turkey, Italy, Chile and Argentina. With over a thousand centers dotting the map, we felt for the first time the need to contain our growth.

Actually, my original goal was to sell a dozen franchises. I considered that not only achievable, but about all the market would allow. Mary was delighted the day we signed the papers for Number 11. She had a friend who was active on the social scene and given to detailed accounts of the trips and parties and luxuries she and her husband enjoyed. Mary couldn't wait to tell her that we now had eleven centers.

In reality, we had only eight. A fellow walked in and requested the number 11, and we gladly accommodated him.

We feel a particular debt to the early franchise owners who gambled on an idea and a hot-tempered dreamer.

BUD'S BUSINESS DOZEN   **#4**

You are more than
the number
on the readout
of a
bathroom scale.

Among them was Speedy Kaplan, a kind of Yiddish leprechaun, who came to know more about Kwik Kopy than I did.

In 1960 Speedy's business was floundering. His attorney had advised him to take bankruptcy, but like many of his generation he found the idea repugnant. Out of curiosity, he asked how much a bankruptcy would cost. The attorney told him $700.

"It doesn't matter," said Speedy. "I can't even raise that much. If I had $700 I'd use it for working capital."

He went home to talk to his wife, Sophie, and they held each other and cried. They were going to fold the business. Then, out of the blue, he decided to give me a call. We were total strangers but he had heard that I had helped another printer meet his note by buying some of his equipment. "He helped one," Speedy recalls thinking. "Maybe he would help another."

He introduced himself and asked if he could drive to Houston and see me. He said he needed advice. I didn't ask him any questions. It would have seemed rude. We agreed to meet at nine o'clock that Saturday morning, and as an afterthought I told him to bring his family.

The Gulf Freeway connects Galveston to Houston, fifty miles apart. He was two hours late. His water pump failed and his car broke down. A proud man, already low on hope, Speedy was a wreck when he finally reached my shop.

Speedy was one of the great nonstop talkers. He once gave a seminar in Las Vegas, and the sponsors had to ask him to sit down after eight hours. "I just kept winding myself up," he said later. "I was using flip cards on a tripod. They told me enough was enough."

BUD'S BUSINESS DOZEN   **#5**

The problem with advice
is that the person
who has the answer
doesn't have the problem.

He had to call me twice for directions, and I was waiting in my doorway when he drove up. I gave Speedy my chair and pulled up another for Sophie. Their two little boys, Leon and Frank, wandered around the shop. I only had two chairs, so I pulled up a couple of Coca-Cola boxes and sat down.

I don't tell this story to evoke violin music. It is simply about being civil and the way people should treat each other. Galveston was a city in pain in the early 1960s, an island with an eroding beach and nothing else to attract the tourists. Speedy said, "I've been biting the bullet the last four or five years. I've got loans that the bank refinanced, and for some reason I owe more now than I did before. I can't meet my payments. I love printing. I devote eighteen to twenty hours a day to my business, seven days a week, and I don't know why I can't make it."

When I said I would try to help, Sophie started crying so hard that her tears actually splattered on the desk. I said, "Just a minute, honey. Don't do that. I don't own that desk."

My business wasn't in great shape either, but if I had learned anything I had learned how to cut costs. I drove to Galveston and looked at Speedy's equipment. I asked him to write up an inventory of what he had. We were going to hold a garage sale. I printed a brochure and sent one to every printer in Texas. The prices were fair, and he wound up with something like $24,000 in cash.

He was able to pay all his creditors except the bank, and I asked my accountant to audit his loan. It turned out that their rates amounted to usury. By the time the negotiations were over they settled the note for $6,000. He was practically debt-free.

BUD'S BUSINESS DOZEN   **#6**

Quit thinking about thinking to quit.

I had no angle. I wasn't looking for a commission. One day Speedy took a diamond ring off his finger, the only real asset he had. "I know it's worth $5,000," he said. "I know you'd do the same." I was moved by the gesture, but I wouldn't take it.

Once he was rid of all the surplus equipment that had been bleeding him, his print shop began to turn a small profit. We began to meet every Saturday just to have lunch and talk about the problems of the universe.

I was able to help the Kaplans because my nature demands action and that was what they needed. Not empty words. They needed answers right away. Problems are like rust; they never sleep.

Speedy was still rebuilding when I started to franchise the Kwik Kopy centers. He saw the phone number on a billboard one day driving into Houston; he didn't even know I was part of Kwik Kopy.

I wasn't at all sure my friend could afford the risk of owning one. I checked him out. It's like playing poker with your brother. You trust him, but you still cut the cards.

I found out that when his father died, Speedy paid off his indebtedness. This was a decent man. The first Kwik Kopy franchise sold outside Houston went to Speedy Kaplan. He paid off the franchise fee at a hundred dollars a month.

His sons Leon and Frank, and Frank's wife, Arriene, run the center now. They accepted the award when Speedy was honored at our annual conference in 1990. Speedy was in the hospital in Galveston, and we said a prayer that night for his recovery. Against the odds, his condition improved and he went home; he was up and down in 1991. But halfway into 1992 he was still active, writing

• • • • • • • • • • • • • • • • • • • •

I have no use for
parasites,
and the eagle is the
antithesis of a
parasite. It fights for
what it gets. The
eagle is what
America is all about.

• • • • • • • • • • • • • • • • • • • •

articles for our magazine, *Kwik Kopy Kids,* and still drumming up ideas to help his business—and ours. Priceless are the friends who can make our spirits soar.

It is no coincidence that the corporate symbol of Kwik Kopy is the American bald eagle. I have what may be one of the country's most complete collections of eagle imagery: paintings, etchings, stained glass, sculptures. There are about a thousand eagle images in the main office building alone.

I have always been an independent sort. I have no use for parasites, and the eagle is the antithesis of a parasite. It fights for what it gets. The eagle is what America is all about. I have very little patience with idiots who run America down; we are a great country. A litigious country, as I learned from firsthand experience, but nevertheless a great one.

Chapter

4

The Lawsuit

• •

Stay out of the courthouse.
Even if you win the case,
you end up a loser.
Only the lawyer gets paid
for his time
before the judge.

• • • • • • • • • • • • • • • • • • • •

N
o matter how people phrase the question—
what was the most exciting or unforgettable moment in
Kwik Kopy's history?—my answer requires no hesitation
and is always the same.

It was the day I learned the company was being sued
for $63 million. Actually, I fudge the number slightly to
make the answer more dramatic, although, at the time, I
can honestly say the news had about all the drama I could
stand.

It began when a disgruntled franchise owner persuaded a number of other owners to join him in a $21
million suit, with treble damages. They sued under the
RICO provision of the law. In case the term isn't familiar to
you, and I hope there is no reason it should be, this is the
statute the Justice Department had enacted to more easily
prosecute the Mafia and other elements of organized crime,
including drug traffickers.

Unfortunately, this is the company in which Kwik
Kopy was lumped. It isn't easy to be objective about a firm
one has built from the ground up, but I can tell you this;
the only time we get our hands dirty is when touching

• • • • • • • • • • • • • • • • • •

Greed is even more

contagious than fear.

• • • • • • • • • • • • • • • • • •

printer's ink. Within our industry, Kwik Kopy had an image about as threatening as the New Christy Minstrels.

I can spin a joke about the suit now. I occasionally boast that we emerged stronger and more secure as a result of it. I do believe that until you have been tested, you can't know what kind of character you and your employees have. We found out. We were tested. And, at the time, I was angry, worried, bitter, fearful, uncertain, a walking ball of barbed wire. The thought of losing your company and good people losing their jobs does that to you.

And while I knew, and our attorneys kept reminding me, that the RICO charge was purely a legal maneuver, a form of intimidation, I hated the very nastiness of it. My blood boiled. Nor was the irony lost on me. We were in this situation for two reasons: (1) we were right, and (2) I'm stubborn.

I would not overlook or compromise an act of outright dishonesty. It was that simple.

A franchise owner in Atlanta had been stealing our royalties. (That was how I put it; the attorneys would prefer that we say that he refused to make his full royalty payment.) He had, in fact, devised a scheme to avoid them. He opened a second printing center and contended that whatever work passed through there was unrelated to his Kwik Kopy franchise.

It was clear what he was doing, and I made one last attempt on the phone to resolve the matter. He said, "Look, I'll tell you what I'm going to do. If you try to pursue this, I'm going to hire a lawyer and I'm going after YOU guys."

He filed suit and so did we. Fair enough. What we did not anticipate was that his lawyer would fan out across the country, cajoling and recruiting other owners to join in the

• • • • • • • • • • • • • • • • • • • •

Indecision is an insult to

progress.

When it's time to make

a decision about a person

or a problem...

trust your intuition

...act!

• • • • • • • • • • • • • • • • • • • •

action. The story his lawyer told was this: If you owe Kwik Kopy money, we can get it wiped out. We're going to sue them. The potential damages, tripled, will amount to $63 million. You can share in that money. We make a good deal, you make a good deal. No more royalties. No more payments.

I learned that greed is even more contagious than fear. They enlisted sixty-two owners to take part in the suit, nearly 10 percent of our franchises at that time. I was more than disappointed. I took it like a knife in my heart. We helped some of those owners become millionaires.

We quickly began to call the other owners. The letters and faxes poured in from the owners who refused to be seduced. A majority, by far, remained loyal and sympathetic. But our troubles were heightened by the number who decided to straddle the fence, who wouldn't join the suit and decided, well, if the ship is going to sink, why should we pay royalties? So they withheld their payments, and our problems began to snowball. The financial noose tightened day by day.

By February 1985, we had finished construction and moved into our new campus at Northwest Forest, a major investment. We were no longer cash heavy, but we had the wind under our wings, with centers and profits steadily increasing. We started to look more closely at inquiries from beyond our borders.

Now, suddenly, we had to do some really innovative financing to stay alive. The expense of the lawsuit, the loss of the revenues, quickly cleaned out our cash reserves. We tabled any thoughts of expansion. We put aside any long-term planning.

From the start, I understood the seriousness of the law-

• • • • • • • • • • • • • • • • • • • •

What is black and tan and

looks good on a lawyer?

A doberman.

• • • • • • • • • • • • • • • • • • • •

suit. At no time did any one of us who dealt with it under-estimate the dangers. But I must say that a heavy burden fell on Steve Hammerstein, who had joined the company as the vice president of legal affairs in January 1984. Within two years he moved up to president. Once an engineer with RCA in Ohio, Steve obtained his law degree and moved to Houston, keeping a promise to his Texas-born wife. He went into practice with his brother-in-law, whose clients included Kwik Kopy.

Hiring Steve was one of my shrewder moves. This is how Steve remembers it:

"I started working on the Kwik Kopy account in 1979. The first year, I worked on the FTC rule that requires franchises to make a disclosure, or an offering circular. I was involved in preparing those documents, franchise agreements, and some of the disputes that surfaced from time to time.

"I didn't have much contact with Bud. I dealt mostly with their in-house counsel, with Mary Lou White, who was in charge of franchise services, and Hiram Downard, who had the title of president until his death in a car accident. Bud grieved a long while over Hiram's death.

"I found out later that Bud had been watching me. He's an observer. I was walking out of Kwik Kopy one night, loaded down with two boxes of records I needed to prepare documents. Admittedly, I wasn't in a good mood. It was the end of a long day and I was tired. Bud and I happened to walk out at the same time. He said 'hello' as I put the boxes down to shake hands. He struck up a conversation, in his fashion. Somehow he knew I was interested in horses—I don't remember telling him.

"He said, 'Steve, instead of being a jockey, have you

• • • • • • • • • • • • • • • • • • •

To my mind, there is no greater waste of time than to engage in a lawsuit, nothing more likely to inspire rage and pure, unadulterated venom.

• • • • • • • • • • • • • • • • • • •

ever thought about being a trainer?' I liked the symbolism. I said, 'That's an interesting analogy.' He said, 'If you ever want to change jobs, let me know.' I said something to the effect that he had my interest, and he said, 'Let's go talk.'

"We didn't talk long because at the time I was a municipal court judge and I had court duty. We went to his townhouse, which happened to be on my way, and we talked. That was basically when he offered me the position of vice president of legal. I would say it was one of Bud's typical ways of operating. He surprises you. I think sometimes he surprises himself.

"I left RCA because I didn't like the corporate life. I didn't like the way they treated their older engineers. I looked to the future and saw a gold watch and a handshake. That didn't seem to be the way I wanted to contribute. That was why I went into law. Not to make a point of how naive I was, but in my first trial I had the second chair, and a witness was on the stand for the other side. I turned to the attorney sitting next to me and said with complete sincerity and shock, 'She's lying!' He literally laughed out loud. We almost disrupted the trial.

"Over the long term, I was having second thoughts about practicing law. I said I wouldn't work for a corporation, but I knew Kwik Kopy and liked the people. I liked the way they operated. I knew the atmosphere and was comfortable with it. And I was coming in as a vice president. In the back of my mind, I thought, maybe I won't be in law the rest of my life if this opens up a new vista."

We were preoccupied with the suit for almost a year to the day, but it seemed like a lifetime. Normally, I express my affection for lawyers in the following joke: What is black and tan and looks good on a lawyer? A doberman.

BUD'S BUSINESS DOZEN   **#7**

Expect
the
unexpected.

But at Kwik Kopy we have had some of the best. Steve is a sensitive fellow, and part of his job was to translate what the other lawyers were saying—their theory of the case, the depth of our exposure—in a way that would not send me howling into the night.

To my mind, there is no greater waste of time than to engage in a lawsuit, nothing more likely to inspire rage and pure, unadulterated venom. Having said that, I think of the alternative. Putting aside moral judgment, I might have said of our bandit in Atlanta, "Okay, I'll let it go. The amount involved won't justify the aggravation." Certainly, from a dollars-and-cents standpoint, the company would have come out well ahead. The decision we made wasn't meant to be punitive. It was dictated by a basic business principle: You can't permit one renegade to violate his contract and withhold his payments and expect those who play by the rules and who stick by you to feel they have been treated fairly. Our revenue stream depended on those royalties. You must be consistent if you plan to stay in business. And besides, I don't like liars.

Still, knowing you are right, believing strongly that you will win, doesn't make the hard times any easier to stomach. I tend to be outspoken. Steve Hammerstein has said of me, "Bud does a lot of thinking and shares those thoughts at various stages of development."

During that year, I had a lot more time to think. I did a lot less sleeping. I tried to remind myself that the issue was not personal, but one that went to the heart of how we operate. Many a night, studying the ceiling, I wondered what the outcome would be. When you are hit with a lawsuit that seeks up to $63 million in damages, you have to recognize that Dame Justice is blind. We could be morally right and lose the suit. We could win the battle

BUD'S BUSINESS DOZEN **#8**

Never promise
what you can't
deliver.

and lose the war. We were on our backs, and our legal bills kept mounting. Royalties were dribbling in. Even if we won, would we be too wounded to survive?

That was easily the worst period of my life. Each month we have a company meeting, and I report to our employees on whatever is going on. How do you tell more than one hundred hard-working, neat people, that they are being sued, that their bosses are accused of being racketeers? The suit charged deceptive trade practices and threw in a RICO claim with no basis at all, pretty much for the nuisance value. They risked nothing.

Our business fell off so sharply that I took a step I would never have considered. I brought in a business consultant. The first time we sat down, he said he could save me $300,000 a year. I needed that savings badly. "Can you do that," I asked, "without firing employees?"

"Oh, yes," he said.

"I don't understand how."

"We'll show you," he said.

They brought in a whole crew of Ivy League MBA's who spent a couple of weeks with us. They poked into every corner of the company, and they transferred their findings to charts. One fellow held up a chart, I'm not kidding, that was the length of our boardroom. He had all these wiggly lines representing all the things that had gone wrong. I fell asleep during their presentation. Someone would nudge me, but I kept nodding off.

I told the consultant, "Look, you can't help me." I told him to gather up his people and take a walk. He never did show me how he was going to save us that $300,000 without layoffs. When I told him we couldn't use him, he went from being very warm and fatherly to meaner than

BUD'S BUSINESS DOZEN **#9**

Your worst employee—
too good to fire
and not good enough
to keep.

hell. To make matters more unpleasant, we still had to let seventeen employees go to meet the payroll. We tend to think that consultants can give us the magic words. But they can't. He was just another guy trying to sell a load of fertilizer.

Meanwhile, attorneys for both sides were taking depositions around the country. If we made any tactical error, it was in not reacting sooner and sending an attorney on the road to explain our position to the franchise owners, in particular to the ones who were wobbling. As we deposed more owners, our confidence grew.

At last the case went into pretrial hearings in Atlanta, and a federal judge ruled in our favor on virtually every point. He made it clear that he was going to throw out most of their complaints. In the end, the attorneys got together and a settlement was more or less brokered by the judge. On its face, the judgment very clearly absolved Kwik Kopy of any wrongdoing, denied all of the allegations in the plaintiffs' petition, and awarded Kwik Kopy compensation in the amount of $725,000.

Every penny we collected went to legal fees, accounts payable, and to pay off the interest on loans. The suit wracked us for three years. We labored to get our employees motivated again, and to bring our recalcitrant owners back into the fold. None of it was easy.

Although I felt vindicated, there was no time for gloating. We had defended a point that was crucial to us. Franchise companies such as Kwik Kopy depend to a large extent on loyalty. You can enforce your relationships with contracts, but in the end you have to believe in the honor system (but not the Tooth Fairy). If there isn't respect and good will and even some mild affection, the company can't withstand the normal shocks of business.

● ●

You can enforce
your relationships
with contracts,
but in the end
you have to believe
in the honor system
(but not the tooth fairy).

● ● ● ● ● ● ● ● ● ● ● ● ● ● ● ● ● ● ● ●

I have never been a vengeful or spiteful person, but I was willing to make an exception this time. I decided that I was going to open up a new center next to each store that went against us and break them. Then I picked up a pencil and put it down on paper, the way I did when we first started out. The plan stopped right there because we didn't have the money to put it in motion. I'm glad it couldn't work.

I kept thinking. I am not what most people would call a very religious person, but I know a few passages from the Bible. The one I kept recalling was, "Vengeance is mine, sayeth the Lord." I thought, okay, I'll buy that. How can I exact my revenge without wallowing in something wicked? I had to find a reason for what happened.

My emotional response to the suit was to recognize it for what it was: nonsense and greed. But if sixty-three of our franchise owners were willing to gang up on us, there had to be something else involved. If we had been doing our jobs as well as we honestly thought we were, the loyalty would have held. It hadn't. I needed to look at the lawsuit as the product of something we were not doing right, or doing enough of. One area seemed obvious: we just were not communicating. That could be corrected.

I resolved to make Kwik Kopy so strong, so good, so profitable that every owner who left the system would one day say, "That was the worst business decision I ever made." This approach was a much healthier one. We would raise our sights rather than tear others down.

From that point on, we turned it around. I firmly believe we now do more for our owners than an overwhelming majority of franchisers in any field. At the time we were sued, roughly 80 percent of our income was generated by new center sales. Royalties made up the

• •

*Winning breeds
complacency. To avoid
that trap requires a
constant vigil.*

• •

other 20 percent.

Today 82 percent of our income is from royalties, and less than 20 percent comes from everything else.

When Kwik Kopy passed the one-thousand-center mark, I put a hold on opening new outlets. "Our goal," I announced, "isn't to go on to two thousand, but to be sure that the thousand we have are strong and successful." When we have accomplished this, we will take a hard look at the next challenge.

The next challenge was the founding of the International Center for Entrepreneurial Development (ICED). With its founding we had the opportunity to acquire The Ink Well of America. Like Kwik Kopy, The Ink Well is a franchisor of quick-printing centers. The marriage between Kwik Kopy and The Ink Well works because we share the basic philosophy of unlimited support to the franchise owners.

The lawsuit left scars. We exercised a provision in our contract that allowed us to expel the owners who had banded together. Some called and some wrote letters saying they had been misled or sweet-talked into joining the suit. Many pleaded to come back. I insisted that every call and every letter be directed to my desk. And I personally told them, not only no, but hell no, they were no longer affiliated with Kwik Kopy and there would be no exceptions.

Later, we did some tracking to see how many of those owners stayed in the printing business. Over half were no longer in operation. I take no satisfaction in whatever hardships were caused. But I don't mind saying that many had convinced themselves that all they were getting from us was a name and a logo. They discovered, too late and to

● ● ● ● ● ● ● ● ● ● ● ● ● ● ● ● ● ● ● ●

You're doing everything
possible for your
customers. Right?
Wrong!!
The road to improvement
is always under
construction.
And, it never ends.

● ● ● ● ● ● ● ● ● ● ● ● ● ● ● ● ● ● ● ●

their regret, that there was much more available in our support system.

That costly episode taught us not to let down our guard. Winning breeds complacency. To avoid that trap requires a constant vigil. Before the lawsuit, we thought our job performance was fine. However, someone convinced those sixty-two owners that it wasn't. I regarded many of those people as friends. And some we had nursed through lean times. I still don't fully understand their disloyalty, but I no longer dwell on it. I am too busy dwelling on the vow I made: To do our job so well, no one ever again will be able to talk our people into a class action suit.

There is a story that merits telling here.

Two years after Ronald Reagan left office, the former president spoke (along with Dr. Peale) at our 1990 Annual International Conference. We shook hands backstage and chatted for a few minutes. My first impression of him was one of mild surprise. He was six-feet tall, very trim and athletic-looking. Not short, not slight, yet I always envisioned him as about six-foot-eight. It seems strange to say it, but he is the kind of person who, after you have known him a few minutes, you feel as if you want to protect him. He is an endearing man of influence, who had that effect on me.

Which led me to a question I had long wanted to ask. I had read virtually every book about Reagan I could get my hands on, including the one by Maureen Reagan, *First Father, First Daughter*. Next to Nancy, I suppose Maureen is his most unabashed defender. At the mention of her book, he cocked his head and looked at me a bit quizzically. She had described some of his disappointments, the people who had been close to him and later let him down, or so she felt.

• • • • • • • • • • • • • • • • • • • •

*The biggest mistake you
can make in business is
losing faith in people.
Don't let a few who
lie or backstab
screw up your future.
Just because you get
poison ivy is no reason to
chew up the leaves.*

• • • • • • • • • • • • • • • • • • • •

I said, "President Reagan, I have only one question. It's about something that you do well, and I'd like to understand how you do it. You never seem to let circumstances get the best of you, even when people you have trusted stab you in the back. I have a temper, and I'm still working on it, but I've never been able to handle disloyalty. You don't hold any animosity, and I'm curious how you handle it."

He motioned me away from the Secret Service agents and the circling crowd. We found a quiet corner where he told me that his father had been an alcoholic and he would often have to help carry him to bed. When he was still too young to understand it, his mother took him aside and tried to explain his father's behavior. She said, "Don't be angry or upset with him. Don't judge him. Drinking is a sickness, and he can't always help the things he does." They were going to love him anyway. That was the way his mother taught him to look at his father's weakness.

And all these years later, if someone disappoints him, he doesn't let it bother him. Disloyalty is a form of sickness too. "Sometimes," said Ronald Reagan, "they just can't help it." Isn't that, I ask you, a forgiving philosophy?

As we walked back to the other guests, he said, matter of factly, "I like people." I found it quite easy to believe that he does. His words helped reinforce a conviction that had taken me time to accept. The biggest mistake you can make in business is losing faith in people. Don't let a few who lie or backstab screw up your future. Just because you get poison ivy is no reason to chew up the leaves. When he met my wife, Mary, and my son, Jimmy, he was gracious and witty. He looked at Jim, a strapping six-foot-five, and quipped, "Boy, you're a block off the old chip."

On a slightly smaller scale, our Canadian licensees went through the same bloody experience in 1990. Forgive

• • • • • • • • • • • • • • • • • • • •

The challenge is to build.
That's why franchising is
wonderful. You see
somebody who is scared
and intimidated and in
two years they have a
thriving company: they
have succeeded
beyond their expectations.

• • • • • • • • • • • • • • • • • • • •

The American eagle is the symbol of Kwik Kopy. The indomitable spirit of this great bird exemplifies the entrepreneurial drive that has brought Bud Hadfield's dream to fruition. This classic example, which stands in the foyer of the Administration Building, was carved out of camphor wood by Thai craftsmen.

Clothed in ivy, the Administration Building blends perfectly into the pastoral landscape.

Flags of every nation hosting a Kwik Kopy presence make a splash of vivid color against the surrounding green.

Visitors to Northwest Forest are welcomed by a majestic statue of a bald eagle, carved by an artist with a chainsaw out of solid oak.

Tall iron gates open onto a courtyard of flowers, filled with the soft music of a fountain.

The Alamo occupies a special place in the hearts of all who believe that every man should walk proud and free. As our training facility, the Alamo at Northwest Forest fulfills this glorious tradition.

Inside the Alamo, a spacious atrium serves as a place for seminars, meetings, weddings and banquets. Upstairs rooms are named for Texas heroes.

The lounge at La Hacienda is the perfect place to relax, or even to indulge in the most civilized of customs, la siesta.

La Hacienda, *with its red tile roof and ornate balconies, evokes the timeless spell of Old Mexico. Lodging and meeting rooms are designed to welcome guests.* "Mi casa es su casa."

The cloistered courtyard of La Hacienda is a place where time stands still.

Sturdy log buildings in a woodland setting add a frontier note. The "Log Inn," with its spotless kitchen, is our cafeteria.

"Inn I" is home for new franchise owners, who come to us from around the world for their initial training.

The lounge at "Inn I" is a gathering place for students occupying the ten comfortable apartments. Nothing has been overlooked.

Lighted courts are but one of the amenities at Northwest Forest. Tennis, anyone?

Texas summers get mighty hot. A cooling dip in the pool behind the "Log Inn" is the perfect solution.

Sometimes a little solitude is necessary. Relax by the lake in a shady gazebo.

Until the U.S. Cavalry arrives, our air conditioning system is safe behind the log walls of the stockade.

The streets of our "Western Town" are quiet and peaceful; no gunslingers need apply. Actually, the storefronts are filled with antiques and serve to hide the laundry, storage facility and waste treatment plant.

Built in memory of Hiram Downard, past president of Kwik Kopy who died in 1981, this simple white chapel honors his many contributions.

*Bud Hadfield, Kwik Kopy Founder,
with wife Mary who named Kwik Kopy.*

me if at times I appear to hide behind a third party to make a point, but this is their book, too. So this seems an appropriate spot to bring in Kent Harding, who won his case and gained a fresh perspective of ours:

"In Canada, we opened one hundred and sixteen centers in nine years. Then we took a pause and tried to clean them up and make them better. It doesn't hurt to consolidate now and then. I know the lawsuit was the low ebb for Bud and the company. It was a very critical time for him. The company had gone from fairly small to being a big business. It was profitable, but cash was scarce and there was a dark cloud on the horizon.

"You don't expect people whom you've helped become rich to turn on you. The majority were high-end producers, the ones sending in the big dollars. Now your cash flow is down, and the bankers are asking what is happening. When you have this kind of problem, everyone around you suddenly questions your judgment. You question yourself. Whether you have done anything wrong. Have you been so blinded by the success that you didn't notice the cracks? The thing that is most difficult, and this is my observation, is the fact that your whole career has been one of building.

"I have been in a few businesses in my day, and in each case I built from the start. That's the time when business is the most fun, when you're building. You can hire people to maintain it. The challenge is to build. That's why franchising is wonderful. You see somebody who is scared and intimidated and in two years they have a thriving company: they have succeeded beyond their expectations.

"That's our role. Then all of a sudden a destructive thing happens, and your thinking goes funny. How do you stay positive when all these negative factors are coming at

Please Help Me

Please come into my life—
  but don't try to take over.
Please help me to think—
  but don't try to think for me.
Please help me find a better way—
  but don't expect me to do it your way.
Please help me—even if I'm wrong.
Help me to stand again—
  but don't carry me.
Please help me to move forward again
  even if we move forward
    in different directions.
And—last of all—
  if you can't help me to be
    what I want to be,
  then please don't hurt me
    by trying to make me
      what you expect me to be.

Bud Hadfield

you? The temptation is to turn vengeful. People have tried to ruin you. Now what should you do, try to destroy them instead?

"I'm not an expert at that. I'm an expert at building, and in the end you come back to that. Bud did a marvelous thing. He kept up a strong front to his people, his employees. They get upset and distraught knowing somebody out there is toying with their lives. They go to work and give it everything they have and all of a sudden the malcontents are saying their best isn't good enough. It's rough. You find yourself out there all by yourself.

"The thing I see with Bud is that he became a true professional. He worked harder and harder. He put in super-human hours. He worked from three in the morning to seven or eight at night. He was all business. He really started to build a rock-solid company.

"He doesn't have much tolerance for weaknesses, but if someone has one little ounce of 'try,' he is right there with them. Although he doesn't show much of it, Bud has written some marvelous poetry. One had the theme, 'Please help me, but don't try to take over.' That's Bud.

"There is a natural conflict between the people who have a capacity for mucking things up and those who are creative and positive and optimistic."

Those Canadians have a way with words. I have to forgive Kent for the gag he pulled on me while virtually my entire work force hid in the shadows and watched.

I pass on this vignette in the hope, misguided though it may be, that it reflects an important truth: There is room in the corporate world for a little harmless horseplay. And the automatic response of the boss is not, "Off with their heads!"

• • • • • • • • • • • • • • • • • • • •

Teamwork is among the
most difficult goals to
achieve because people,
like nations, think
individually.

• • • • • • • • • • • • • • • • • • • •

In Harding's defense, he claimed that this elaborate gag was in retaliation for a few minor jokes I had played on him. Perhaps. Still, he took advantage of my concern for the environment, not to mention my sensitive nature.

He knew I had been upset because a water moccasin in the small lake outside our building had been pulling down the baby ducks and drowning them. Once, spotting the struggle of a helpless duckling, I had grabbed my shotgun out of the trunk of my car and fired a shell or two across the lake, hoping to frighten the moccasin. My effort was in vain, but the gunshots did cause a stir around the campus.

On one of his trips to Houston, Kent bought a remote-controlled submarine with an antenna at the top. He then bought a plastic foam snake's head, painted it dark green, and attached it to the antenna.

While I was busy, he went to the lake and tested his equipment. It would actually dive, surface and glide through the water.

The word quickly spread that the next morning, at ten sharp, the hated reptile was going to appear on the lake. Here is Kent, with the rest of the story:

"I had a cohort with me from Canada who was good at operating a radio. We had to sneak around so the gadget would be in direct view from the window of Bud's office on the second floor. At the appropriate time I was with Bud and I pointed out the window and said, 'There's that bloody water moccasin again.'

"With that Bud jumped over a chair, ran into his back room, grabbed his shotgun, stuffed some shells in the pockets of his jumpsuit and in his stocking feet ran down the hallway, heading for the stairs. At which point, the

• • • • • • • • • • • • • • • • • • •

Quit trying to get even,
try getting ahead instead!

• • • • • • • • • • • • • • • • • • •

marketing people were bringing out new prospects considering buying a Kwik Kopy franchise. Someone said, 'Oh, this is our founder, Mr. Hadfield.' Bud panted, 'Can't talk to you right now,' and kept going.

"We hadn't arranged for them to follow along, that was just a bonus to have an audience. Bud continued out the front door with his shotgun, ran to the lake, loaded up, cocked the gun and blew the moccasin's head off. With that the sub surfaced—it looked like a model of a German U-boat—and headed toward us. He was going to blast it again when he realized it was a toy.

"He turned around to see his entire staff peeking out of the windows and cheering. He turned to me, smiled from ear to ear, muttered, 'You so-and-so,' went back to his office and closed the door."

Kent presented me with the submarine as a memento. I keep it on my desk.

Obviously, one of the satisfactions of expanding over-seas is the fact that you can now be sued in different languages. There are other adjustments, of course, and one is the additional emphasis that must be placed on team-work. The word, the idea, is almost a cliché. Yet teamwork is among the most difficult goals to achieve because people, like nations, think individually.

It is instructive for those of us at the Kwik Kopy head-quarters to observe the cultural differences in our interna-tional partners. And, I hope, instructive for them to get to know us.

To this end, we asked Kent Harding's associate, Hugh Marchand, a fellow with a cool, analytical mind, to com-pare those differences. Hugh joined Kwik Kopy Canada more than ten years ago and became its president in 1986.

BUD'S BUSINESS DOZEN   **#10**

Winners *feel* like winners.
Losers *act* like losers.

His background is in accounting, and he has a wide range of experience in the fields of automotive parts, plastics and computers.

At the time he offered his viewpoint he had just returned from an Outward Bound trip in the northernmost wilderness of Canada. By the luck of the draw, he was the only male in a group that included six women. Guys with the darkly handsome looks of a French racecar driver tend to have this kind of luck, or so it seems. Marchand said the experience of seeing how a female-dominated group worked was fascinating, and I have no reason to doubt him. "I realized that my training had always been linear," he said. "I came from an environment that said if you have a problem, you examine it exhaustively, assign responsibility, assign priorities and get on with it. What I found with these women was a different, almost chaotic way of doing things. You almost go into a consensus mode. Decisions were arrived at almost by osmosis. Everyone went off and had their roles.

"I was struck by their ability not to need a beginning and an ending. I suppose this is a roundabout way of getting to the point, but this is what I have found in Bud. He has a huge wealth of information at his fingertips. He has this ability to plunge right in, to shuffle the pieces, to say this is a more interesting combination."

It is still not clear to me why, when we asked him to talk about Kwik Kopy and Canada, Hugh was reminded of his survival test with six active, healthy young women. But he sort of went from there, no holds barred:

"There is a matter of national pride involved here. And, I probably should preface this by saying that it is unlikely I could work for Bud. In terms of style, ours is contradictory. This has nothing to do with personal affec-

• • • • • • • • • • • • • • • • • • •

If you run a company, you
want to know what the
scouting reports say.
Are you out of touch?
Have your ideas gotten stale?
The rest doesn't much
matter. It isn't important
that you believe
the nice words—as long
as they do.

• • • • • • • • • • • • • • • • • • •

tion. He has always respected the fact that we operate in a different environment.

"The first major difference is the profile of the owners. In Canada, our owners, by and large, come from middle management backgrounds. They are more likely to be professionals, on balance probably more university educated. The average age of the Canadian owner would be less than the Americans. We would have fewer retirees. In some ways, our owners are probably critical more quickly.

"Canadians don't much wave the Maple Leaf. In a situation such as Kwik Kopy, where so much of the culture is wrapped up in the flag, where Bud is an unashamed patriot, that doesn't cut much ice in Canada. Most Canadian owners, one should add, hold Bud in very high regard. They respect his achievement as the founder of an obviously successful business. They are probably a bit overawed by the Americanism of the business.

"Where it becomes interesting is when most of them go to Houston and get drawn out of their shells. Everything is so up, so positive. They come back thinking, 'I know this is hype, but maybe I need to be hyped.' They don't lose that enthusiasm, but it suffers a sea change when they come home.

"We find Americans generous in their praise, Canadians a little less so. That skepticism makes our job somewhat harder. There is a slightly more cynical view here. If an owner does well, he did it himself. If he fails, that sorry Kwik Kopy is at fault. We have some of that attitude to counter.

"To begin with, there is a tremendous U.S. investment in Canada. So many people who work in industry have worked in a branch plant, which can be a very frustrating

• • • • • • • • • • • • • • • • • • •

The more the
company grows,
the more it will be
tested.

• • • • • • • • • • • • • • • • • • •

experience in the sense that you don't get access to the full range of management decisions. This is probably true worldwide.

"One of the really good things about Kwik Kopy is that the company takes a more open approach. No one is excluded from the process. Ambition is vigorously encouraged. The more the company grows, the more it will be tested. While Bud has developed a unique business system with a strong emphasis on keeping the model the same, that will get strained in years to come when you have German and French and Italian owners going to Houston, with their Prussian, Gallic and Roman attitudes. There has never been an insistence that you export the U.S. model. Unwittingly or not, this is a very smart move. In Canada, we are so alike the differences can be minor. Even so, trying to drop a complete system into place, without allowances for national character, can be harmful. Kwik Kopy recognizes this. Nonetheless, there is a unified philosophy.

"At the root of all this is Bud's ability to think laterally. In my mind this is his strength. This technique epitomizes his way of working. If Bud is preparing a seminar, he uses his famous little cards, and what comes out is almost stream-of-consciousness. He writes on the cards, keeps pondering, writes something else, and quite literally starts to shuffle the cards. He puts them out on the table, all the facts germane to the argument. What he concludes is that the obvious sequence may not be the best way to present it."

There is a risk in offering space in your book to someone else. You may appear to be hiding behind their kindness, fishing for compliments. Still, the quotes are here, unedited. Not all of them are flattering, and that goes in,

BUD'S BUSINESS DOZEN **#11**

Criticism is easy;
achievement
is more difficult.
—Winston Churchill

too. If you run a company, you want to know what the scouting reports say. Are you out of touch? Have your ideas become stale? The rest doesn't much matter. It isn't important that you believe the nice words—as long as they do.

Chapter

5
The Sweat
Hogs

• • • • • • • • • • • • • • • • • • • •

One must never mistake
the silence of the forest for
the absence of activity.

• • • • • • • • • • • • • • • • • • • •

After a night of shop talk during a company field trip, one of our top people, the distinctively named Pattie Paddy, said, "I'm tired of hearing about the $63 million lawsuit. It's so negative."

I disagreed. "No," I said. "It really isn't. It was one of the best things that ever happened to us and not just because we won. It surely did shake up my thinking. It completely rewired my head."

I am even tempted to use the fancy word, paradigm, meaning that my brain has a new format.

Certainly, I had found contentment with the rate of our growth and was feeling temporarily godlike. Many in the company, it appeared, shared my exhilaration.

We were blind, if not actually stupid, about what was going on beyond our orbit. One must never mistake the silence of the forest for the absence of activity. In an organization that had become as far-flung as ours, somewhere, people had to have some secret dissatisfactions. Right or wrong, they had to have them. Nor was it their responsibility to tell us they were unhappy. It was our responsibility to find out.

• • • • • • • • • • • • • • • • • • •

Perceptions are more real

than reality itself.

• • • • • • • • • • • • • • • • • • •

This soul-searching led directly to the creation of the Sweat Hogs, one of the most productive ideas we ever implemented. The first day I pulled in a team of people and called them Sweat Hogs, they all gagged. They hated the name. The name, of course, was adapted from the television sitcom, *Welcome Back, Kotter.* Now, to become a Sweat Hog at Kwik Kopy, you have to be voted in by your peers. It's like being inducted into an honor society. They are extremely proud of it; they have little pig figurines all over the place.

In actuality, unless our franchise owners called us, we didn't know how they were faring. And I knew, or should have known, from my days at sea that when you are cut off from the home port you tend to sit out there and let small grievances escalate. Some people like to moan and groan. Real or imagined, perceptions can change. I drew a valuable conclusion a long time ago: Perceptions are more real than reality itself. We deal with reality, but we are influenced by perception. In the long haul perception will change all your thinking. If one thing is wrong, everything is wrong, because you perceive it that way.

In reality, one thing is wrong, you correct it and everything is fine.

That day I said, "Every month we need to talk to every franchise owner." We started out calling them Happy Calls, which sounded like a song from *South Pacific.* We used that label for a few months and ash-canned it. If an owner gets up in the morning, has a fight with his or her spouse, gets a ticket on the way to work, has a flat tire, walks in the door to find the office manager has quit, picks up a phone and hears a cheery voice say, "This is your happy call!" you are not off to a good start.

There was no book on this procedure. To my knowl-

• • • • • • • • • • • • • • • • • • •

When you're too busy for your customers...don't worry about it. In time you won't be busy at all!

• • • • • • • • • • • • • • • • • • •

edge nobody had ever done this kind of stroking before, so we invented the cog as the wheel rolled along. When we call, we must have a purpose. And we couldn't just say, "Hi, it's nice to talk to you." And we couldn't have too many goals or we would confuse them.

I wanted to keep the goals specific. We now refer to them as Action Calls. First off, we ask, "Are you all right? Do you need anything? Give me one thing to do for you."

Which means that whatever the franchise owner says goes straight into the computer to make sure that we do it. Then we may tell them about an upcoming seminar, one that would interest them in a direct way. The last thing we say is, "Give me a rating (on this call), one being low, ten being the top."

Currently, the Sweat Hogs are at about 9.018 on an average of one to ten. I doubt that there are five other franchises in America that can get that kind of rating from its clients. If an owner says, "Oh, take an eight or a nine," we always report the low side. We don't split the difference and give ourselves an eight and a half.

Occasionally, a caller will get a two or a three as a rating. There are usually eight people in the Franchise Services/Sweat Hogs department and I meet with them for fifteen to thirty minutes every morning at 7:45. We also have over fifty Action Callers company-wide. They want to help. One of my problems is not letting them get ground under by the fallout factor. One day the person on the other end of the line may be really upset about something and the caller will take a hit. Many times it has nothing to do with us. Not long ago we had an owner whose press operator quit. When one of our ladies asked, sweetly, "Give me something I can do for you," he snarled, "Send me a press operator and get him here this morning."

• • • • • • • • • • • • • • • • • • • •

The customer is no longer

king…

The customer is now

the dictator.

• • • • • • • • • • • • • • • • • • • •

We can't and don't provide technical help to solve temporary, everyday problems. We are unable to provide a staff that large. On the other hand, if there is a death in the family or a serious illness, we put someone on a plane that day. As soon as we learn they need help, we send someone to manage the center, run the press or work the counter. They stay as long as they are needed.

But the morale of the Sweat Hogs does need a boost now and then when they have been catching the brunt of those long distance blues. As a group they are quality people, whose generosity is tested when they wind up with someone who is feeling hostile. One owner gave the caller a *zero* and said, "When you fire Steve Hammerstein, I'll rate you better."

One of them called me aside and told me what happened, adding that they would be careful not to bring it up in the meeting.

"Bring it up in the meeting!" I said, with one of my not-too-infrequent growls. I knew that Steve would be there, and I went on, "If you left it up to me, I wouldn't have any patience with an idiot like that. I'd tell him to get out of the system. But you people will swing him around. I know you will."

They were working on turning him around, even though he probably couldn't remember why he was angry at Steve. The funny thing is, more people in the company like Steve than they do me.

I am partial to sporting analogies and this is one that I use to explain Steve's position. I loved to watch Roger Staubach fade back to pass in his prime years with the Dallas Cowboys. But one time he caught a horrific lick and wound up with a concussion. That hardly seemed

• • • • • • • • • • • • • • • • • • •

*The responses we get to
our well-meaning Action
Calls are not always fair,
but that doesn't provide
us with an excuse to quit.*

• • • • • • • • • • • • • • • • • • •

fair, certainly not to Roger, but it was part of being a quarterback.

The responses we get to our well-meaning Action Calls are not always fair, but that doesn't provide us with an excuse to quit. The Sweat Hogs are not conditioned that way. I have more admiration for them than anyone else in the company, and they know it.

Once, I marched the entire board of directors into their room so they could sit through a Sweat Hogs' meeting. And when it was over, I turned to the directors and said, "With you people I had the second most important meeting of my day. The most important one was right here."

If the Action Call idea strikes anyone as gimmicky, that notion didn't bother me then and certainly doesn't now. When the calls first started, the franchise owners would often retort, "Gee, I'm going to fall out of my chair, you've actually called me." We may catch a touch of anger now and again, but rarely sarcasm. The Action Calls are now in their fifth year, and they have gained credibility throughout the company. Whatever rating the owner calls out, the Sweat Hogs never say they were given a nine. They say, "I earned a nine." And I can assure you, they earned it.

There is pressure on me to keep coming up with stories for these meetings to shore up the point that the customer is always right. One of my favorites is the one about the big department store in the west, where a man went to the complaint department and objected that the two tires he bought were defective. He couldn't find his receipt. The manager asked how much he paid for them. He told him, and they cut a check on the spot. The punch line is that the store didn't sell tires. But how much mileage—no pun intended—do you suppose they got from that act of generosity?

● ● ● ● ● ● ● ● ● ● ● ● ● ● ● ● ● ● ●

I will sometimes sit at my
desk for hours on end, and
ideas will come to me,
circling my mind
like particles in the air.

● ● ● ● ● ● ● ● ● ● ● ● ● ● ● ● ● ● ●

I will sometimes sit at my desk for hours on end, and ideas will come to me, circling my mind like particles in the air. You appreciate an idea more if you didn't think of it first, partly because you don't have to defend it. But in all honesty, Action Calls had more of an impact on our company than anything else we have tried. I can sit in on their meetings for thirty minutes and leave having been updated on an impressive number of centers.

I may interrupt their reports to fire questions at them. If one says, "I talked to Sue Newell this morning," I may break in with, "What's her husband's name? What city are they in? Do they have a satellite center?" They better know the answers.

I even holler at them, confident that they know I have a feeling for them close to love. Most people may scoff at that; I don't care. I don't require their acceptance to tell them how I feel. A boy tells a girl he loves her, he doesn't want to hear that she thinks he's a creep. You expect people to respond in kind. They may not, and that's all right. I still have my feelings.

I was having lunch one day with our chief financial officer and the presidents and other officers from a group of banks. When a Dallas banker wanted to know the most exciting thing that ever happened to Kwik Kopy, I told the story—again—of the $63 million lawsuit. I added my postscript, that the outcome was especially rewarding because it led us to establish the Sweat Hogs and Action Call program.

Then I looked around the table and asked them how often they called their customers. The bank presidents turned to their vice presidents who turned to each other. No one spoke. I already knew the answer. None did. Why? Because the first time they got a negative reaction the

● ● ● ● ● ● ● ● ● ● ● ● ● ● ● ● ● ● ● ●

Those who have the right

kind of character

don't tremble

at the first sign of

adversity.

● ● ● ● ● ● ● ● ● ● ● ● ● ● ● ● ● ● ● ●

calls would stop.

I am enthralled with this innovation because it represents the qualities everyone in business seeks. Our people persevere. They stick to it. They keep coming back. They have learned that you don't jump over a chasm with two tries. When your assets are low, you tend to be more willing to experiment, even with an instrument as mundane as the telephone.

In the early days, ambition led us to expand and my desire, my totally unreasonable desire to survive, forced us to accommodate that expansion. I wasn't at all thrilled about going international. Today we have no choice. We either go global or drown in our own stupidity. America, obviously, needs to think more about international markets.

One can always rationalize whatever goes awry. I went into business with some of the wrong people at the wrong time. Someone cheated me. But those who have the right kind of character don't tremble at the first sign of adversity. Look at the late Sam Walton. He started with a five-and-dime store and built it into the biggest operation in the country. Sam would walk into a Wal-Mart somewhere, get behind the register and spend a useful hour or so checking out customers.

Every employee at Kwik Kopy has to spend one day a year working in a center. They learn that your feet hurt at the end of the day.

Which brings us back to the Sweat Hogs. They may call a franchise owner at four o'clock in the afternoon and chances are his corns are aching. They deal with it.

On a typical afternoon, they produced a series of reports on how the various centers were meeting the new chemical disposal regulations issued by OSHA. One passed

• •

Courage

is being scared

to death,

but saddling up anyway.

—John Wayne

• •

along word of a new environmental wash that was being tested. Another suggested devoting an entire issue of our company magazine, the *Kwik Kopy Kids*, to environmental safety.

I added my observation: "We are more and more going to use recycled paper and all that. I'm glad that you're sensitive to it because the company is, and we have to be. We can't make a garbage dump out of our world the way we have been doing. We just want to be sure the chemicals are right before we recommend them."

One of our franchise service representatives said she spoke with a franchise owner whose last name she can't say, but she keeps a note in front of her with the name spelled out phonetically. "When I first started calling him," she said, "he had suffered about a year of declining sales. He was very depressed. He was always polite on the phone, but you could tell he was worried about his business.

"He turned to the corporation for help, and one of our center analysts has been working with him for the last eight months. He was on the Leaders-in-Sales report this month. He has totally turned his business around. When I spoke with him, he was very upbeat. He felt supported by the corporation, which, after all, is the purpose of the Action Call program.

"The other thing that was significant, I always asked him if there was anything I could do for him. The answer was always no. Which I took as, maybe not intentionally, an indication that he didn't trust me to do things for him. He didn't feel comfortable enough with me. This time when I called, he asked me for two or three things. I ordered OSHA manuals, sent him wall graphics for his satellite center, and sent him some "Open" signs.

. . . .

The CEO must lead the
charge; this is one
function that cannot
be delegated.
If the man or woman who
holds across-the-board
bottom-line responsibility
and doesn't totally buy
into the program,
it simply won't last.

. . . .

"I think he really trusts us now, and he rated us a nine—I believe we earned a ten. It has been a real transformation with him. He has gone from having a lot of problems to feeling good about what he is doing and doing it well."

For the past several years I have encouraged other businesses to embrace our Action Call program, so far without success. I've tried speeches, seminars, and even hosting representatives from several major corporations, including our good friends at Eastman-Kodak Company. Perhaps it appears too simple, too much surface consideration. I've heard many convincing arguments for it and not one against it. So why doesn't it work for other companies? Possibly we didn't do a good job of explaining how to set up an Action Call program. Once a company begins a program like this, it has to commit itself out of a sincere desire to continue it—no matter what.

Those companies that are curious about the Action Call program might like to note the following suggestions:

1. The CEO must lead the charge; this is one function that cannot be delegated. If the man or woman who holds across-the-board, bottom-line responsibility doesn't totally buy into the program, it simply won't last. Am I asking too much? Possibly so. It all depends on whether or not you're willing to take the time to do it. "I'm too busy," you say. I'm never too busy to serve our franchise owners because *they are our customers.*

Every morning at 7:40 I walk into the franchise services area and sing out, "Good morning, fellow Sweat Hogs." Usually there are eight to twenty-five present. We invite visiting owners, vendor representatives and anyone else

● ● ● ● ● ● ● ● ● ● ● ● ● ● ● ● ● ● ● ●

In the final consideration,

it's up to you to encourage

and challenge your people

to help make it happen.

● ● ● ● ● ● ● ● ● ● ● ● ● ● ● ● ● ● ● ●

who is interested to attend these morning briefings. We try to hold each report to a maximum of a minute, but that doesn't always work. When a Sweat Hog gets excited about a particular call, there's no turning him or her off. Somehow I can find it in my heart to forgive one of our people for telling good news about a customer. They really want to share, and they expect me to be there to listen. I love it!

2. When an Action Call is made, the caller simply asks questions like, "Are you okay? Do you need anything?" Before the call ends we share some last minute Kwik Kopy news and then ask for a rating from one to ten. Occasionally we get a two or three rating. It's then our job to find out why. Often we have a tough time getting a franchise owner to open up. If there's even a slim chance of solving a problem, we'll try. During our morning meetings, other Action Callers make helpful suggestions and go out of their way to help. They do more than listen—they solve problems. Tough ones. Cosmetic efforts with the depth of a mud puddle would kill the whole thing. They give each other substantive help in record time.

3. Somebody has to love the idea as much as the boss does. I'm blessed with Pattie Paddy, vice president of franchise services. Pattie heads up this department with her assistant and our director of franchise services, Robin Averitt. They make quite a team. Pattie's red hair sparkles when she's on the trail of a problem. She makes her position clear, and we all know she's leading us to a solution. Robin is a quiet young lady with an unbelievable sense of organization. She controls the discipline and logistics. Kwik Kopy is blessed to have these two women—they are magnificent.

4. In the final consideration it's up to you to encourage and challenge your people to help make it happen. Your encouragement, with highly visible rewards, can facilitate

• • • • • • • • • • • • • • • • • • • •

*Give the complaint
department to the kid who
doesn't know any better,
or to the old war horse
who couldn't care
any less.
In time, there will be
no more complaints and
no more business to
worry about.*

• • • • • • • • • • • • • • • • • • • •

the success of the Action Call program. It won't happen with your feet under your desk. Go for it and there's a special bonus when you do it.

In less than thirty minutes a day you can inspire your troops and, at the same time, stay abreast of what's going on with your customers.

It's the most productive twenty minutes of my day, every day. What else can I say?

Our Action Callers don't consider themselves as stars —they would rather be starmakers. Which leads into another Kwik Kopy innovation, our Stars Program. When the company grew so quickly, it became a problem to keep up with staffing and new center start-ups. We had three specialists who traveled around the country training the new franchise owners. They helped them unpack the equipment and get ready for opening day.

It was clear that we had to come up with a better solution. I thought about owners who had been in the business for quite some time, and that led to the concept of the "owner-trainer" or Stars Program. The idea was simple, we would use our best and most experienced owners to train newcomers, a service for which they would be well compensated.

The concept not only solved a problem and served to boost self-esteem, it strengthened the idea that Kwik Kopy owners are willing to share with each other. It also conveyed the message that they can get all the expertise they need right inside the family.

Of course, any company regardless of size, may from time to time need a trouble-shooter, or to borrow a baseball analogy, a closer in the bullpen. Someone who can

• • • • • • • • • • • • • • • • • • • •

Bury your ego.

Don't be the star

Be the star maker!

• • • • • • • • • • • • • • • • • • • •

hold a lead or pull you out of a jam.

Ours is Sheldon Rayman, whose Canadian center was number one in sales. As a hard charger with a long and successful entrepreneurial record, his success in this role came as no surprise. In the summer of 1991, I told the Sweat Hogs: "Sheldon has been going into centers that are in trouble, where the moods are negative. He has never complained, never. But, he has said, he'd like to go into a center once in a while where he didn't feel like he was yesterday's garbage." I told the Sweat Hogs about an owner that Sheldon had recently helped out of financial difficulties and added that he has saved many an owner's bacon. But I didn't see him getting credit from us or the owners.

Someone suggested that we call owners he has helped and tell them we want to run an article in the *Kwik Kopy Kids*, called "Thanks, Sheldon" and ask them to share some nice words about Sheldon. The response was overwhelming.

How Sheldon became Kwik Kopy's trouble-shooter is an interesting story. This is how he tells it:

"Eventually, I sold my Kwik Kopy center, took my profits, and moved to Arizona. I had fallen in love with the business brokerage field. I liked the idea of working strictly on commission. You sell, you get paid. You don't sell, you don't get paid. The rightness of that arrangement appealed to me. I quickly learned two lessons; one, that Kwik Kopy had it beat by a long shot. The second was more costly. In Arizona every third person has a real estate license. It is my theory that almost immediately on arriving in Phoenix or Scottsdale or Tucson, people apply for a real estate license and most of them have no idea what they are doing. Deals kept coming to me with no financial statements, no retail

• • • • • • • • • • • • • • • • • • • •

*Don't always insist
on having everything
your way.
Try giving in on all the
little things and insisting
on the big ones.*

• • • • • • • • • • • • • • • • • • • •

sales figures that could be verified, and leases that were not renewable.

"I finally had two choices to face. I could give it another year and lose all of my money, or close the doors and just lose a chunk of it.

"Around this time I was visiting with Bud at his home, and he said, 'Why don't you join Kwik Kopy on a full-time basis and move to Houston? You don't have to give me an answer now. Think about it.'

"I knew my answer, but I didn't know exactly how to phrase it, so I said nothing. When I first moved to Phoenix, that territory was taken and there was no opening for a Kwik Kopy. And neither one of us looked at me as a guy who would be content with a job; unless one that was custom-made happened to come along. I got on the plane and as soon as I landed in Phoenix I sat down and drafted a letter to Bud. I said, in effect, that what I could do best for Kwik Kopy, was to travel around the country, working with centers that are having problems. All I would need was a telephone, a computer and an airport. I had all three in Phoenix.

"On that same plane trip, by coincidence, I picked up a magazine and spotted an article on people who worked out of their homes. It listed some of the advantages over working for a corporation, such as less overhead. Needless to say, when I sealed my letter I enclosed a copy of the article.

"We reached an agreement, and ever since Bud has constantly introduced me as Kwik Kopy's 'only corporate employee who doesn't live in Houston.' I don't know if there is an underlying message in that statement. I only know that I never get tired of hearing it."

Chapter

6

Creative
Management

• •

My guess is that the
scales cost $50, but in
reality it may have cost
him $50 million.

• •

Over thirty years ago, a fellow I knew had a delicatessen, the kind where the walls and counter were covered with yellow Formica. His place was so small, all he served were sandwiches.

All his business was takeout, but people lined up at the counter and out the door to place their orders. He had some sandwiches made up ahead of time, and he passed them across the counter as fast as he could. You would see him grab a big handful of corned beef, roast beef and salami, slap it on the bread, wrap it in waxed paper and slide it into a bag. You had to be careful your jaw didn't lock when you took a bite.

He was so successful that he decided to expand, and he built a restaurant, a real one, twenty times the size of his original deli. The business is still there, these many years later, but it hasn't grown an inch, and I suspect I know why. I stopped in shortly after he opened and took in the scene. The owner was at the cash register, but now he had a man in a white hat behind the counter, putting the meat on a scale. The customers stood there and watched him carefully weigh the meat and take a little off.

• • • • • • • • • • • • • • • • • • • •

The last thing an effective

manager wants is a

textbook answer.

What I expect from our

people, no,

I insist on it, is an

understanding

of our mission.

• • • • • • • • • • • • • • • • • • • •

My guess is that the scales cost $50, but in reality it may have cost him $50 million. If he had kept giving the customers what they wanted, instead of one location—where he skimps on the meat to offset his overhead—he might have a chain of delis all over the country. He was in business before Ray Kroc, selling those thick sandwiches as fast as he could bag them. If he hadn't decided to measure them, there might be corned beef under the golden arches instead of hamburgers.

The moral of the story is this: There is little hope for real growth if you repay the customers' loyalty by teaspooning your services.

Economy and marketing and strategy have their places, but none is a substitute for good will. I can assure you that there is no shortage of would-be strategists. I have found that the most prolific report writers generally have good memories, or they copy what they need out of a textbook. I once had an employee who was completing his MBA, and he gave me a report that contained suggestions on corporate strategy. The material seemed familiar to me, and then I realized most of it was from another company's annual report. I made some notes and called him into my office. I said, "Tell me, what part did you write and what part did you copy?" I decided if this was what he was getting out of his education, I didn't need him.

The last thing an effective manager wants is a textbook answer. What I expect from our people, no, I insist on it, is an understanding of our mission. When you accomplish that, when you can build on it, the joy of communication pops up all over the place. If you can take a statement and make it clear and distinct to the fellow mowing the lawn, then the chief executive officer can understand it too. Beyond that, strategy is how you react day-to-day to each new

• • • • • • • • • • • • • • • • • • • •

Our Mission Statement:

Our most important phone call is from an owner with a problem. Our second most important phone call is from a prospective franchise buyer.

• • • • • • • • • • • • • • • • • • • •

crisis or opportunity. To try and turn this into a textbook definition is hot air. Of course, in academia I would be attacked vigorously for taking this position because hot air is partly what they sell.

Or, as my friend the sandwich maker might say, no matter how thin you slice it, it's still salami.

You can't own or manage or clerk until you know what your mission is. We have a sign that is given to each employee at Kwik Kopy, it says: Our most important phone call is from an owner with a problem. Our second most important call is from a prospective franchise buyer. That is our mission. The owner with a budget problem gets his answer right now; the potential buyer can wait. People argue that this attitude is simplistic. They can argue all they want. It works.

If I had to reduce my management style to one phrase, it would be this: I believe in what works. If I want fantasy, I'll turn on a movie channel.

This is an example from real life: We tell people who take over an existing Kwik Kopy center not to change anything for six months. It takes at least that long to learn how to exercise the power that an owner has. In wise hands, power becomes a servant, not a destructive force. We find that people who have been in business before and then buy one of our existing centers are conscious of this to the point of being reluctant to make decisions.

A longtime friend of mine, Fred Setser, then in his fifties, took over a shop in Tulsa, Oklahoma, with a crew of people who were all in their twenties. His first concern was whether they would stay with him. The first move he made was to listen to their ideas and their concerns. Several years later, the same crew is still with him. He added a second

• • • • • • • • • • • • • • • • • • •

There are some things
that are not meant
to be explained.
Creativity is one of them.
It is a gift, an unlimited
source of power
that can change your life
when you learn how to
harness it.

• • • • • • • • • • • • • • • • • • •

location and more young people to his staff.

Have you ever known a man who had a chance to admire his statue in a park? Of course not, the statues are all of dead people. I have only contempt for people who push around those who can't push back. If I have a point to make, I leave my ego out of it. When I walk into our company cafeteria, I fuss over the three people behind the steam table. I tell them the food is great. They're great. I joke with them. I'm not looking for a "Good Guy" award. I consider that an exercise in power. To plunge into a company or an office and to change this or that, to brand work as unnecessary, all amounts to gross stupidity.

This is a hard lesson to learn, but sound business practices and quality management are not inconsistent with being creative.

There are some things that are not meant to be explained. Creativity is one of them. It is a gift, an unlimited source of power that can change your life when you learn how to harness it. At this very moment, there is within you a bottomless pool of ideas. Hooking one isn't easy. It isn't supposed to be easy. Creativity isn't the same as talent, and it is important to know the difference.

Mozart created his Symphony Number 40 in G Minor. George Solti and the Chamber Orchestra of Europe combined their individual talents to take silent notes from a piece of paper and thrilled their audiences by bringing those notes to life in the form of music.

Without Mozart the creator, Sir George and his talented musicians would have been silent. Without the Chamber Orchestra of Europe or a group of similar design, Mozart's music would have died with him.

The cold reality of all this lies in the fact that in today's

• • • • • • • • • • • • • • • • • •

Nothing kills a new idea

with more accuracy than

procrastination...

to develop an idea you

must listen to the silence

of your mind.

• • • • • • • • • • • • • • • • • • •

world, the men and women who make it big are both the creators and the talent. They write the songs, they play the tune. They create an idea and provide, or recruit, the talent to bring it to life…to turn the wisp of an idea into wealth.

None of us can capture creativity. It happens, usually at inconvenient times. In my case, the creative process brings me out of a deep sleep about an hour or two before my body recognizes that it is time to awaken. I have to fight the sleep. The temptation to put off creativity until later in the day is strong. But to put off the creative process is to deny it. Hasn't that happened to you? A thought slips into your half-conscious mind. You wrestle with whether to roll out of bed and record it. You turn over, pull up the covers and tell yourself, "later." And later you can't remember what it was all about. The thought is gone.

Creative energy is perishable. Too often, it is now or never. So when your moment arrives, *write it down*. It seems like such a meager effort for so much gain. We don't set the rules in the business of being creative. We live by them. We have to act the instant a creative thought reveals itself. Anything less is nothing more than a self-indulgent exercise in daydreaming.

One of the rules is that you must have a sense of urgency. Nothing kills a new idea with more accuracy than procrastination. The practical development of an idea is more difficult, I think, than to deal with the established art forms. A painter can see the colors with his eyes. A musician can experiment with the notes. But to develop an idea you must listen to the silence of your mind.

Add to your idea, or subtract, but do it on paper. A dull pencil is sharper than the best memory. Have you ever noticed how lawyers write down everything on a legal pad as they talk with you? They don't trust facts to their

• • • • • • • • • • • • • • • • • • •

*To be sure, not every idea
is going to rank with the
electric light bulb.
A company can speed
along on silken wings
when it is fueled by small,
innovative ideas that
enhance performance or
efficiency.*

• • • • • • • • • • • • • • • • • • •

memories. An idea is rarer than a fact.

Twenty-five years ago, I had an idea for using small offset presses to turn out printed sheets by the millions, more quickly than ever before. The irony is, I didn't know how to operate the press that spawned a thousand Kwik Kopy centers and made me a millionaire.

I suppose that proves you don't have to be a practitioner to have an idea. Dr. Henry Heimlich, who invented the technique that saves the lives of thousands of people threatened with choking or drowning, has never performed the Heimlich maneuver. Try as I might, I can find no connection between his idea and mine.

I faced a conspicuous lack of enthusiasm in the beginning.

You can't even depend on those closest to you for support. In fact, friends and relatives may be the worst enemies of your discovery. So don't surrender your idea even if encouragement is lacking. Sharpen it, get it ready for delivery, and simply maintain secrecy until the idea gains sufficient strength to be presented properly to someone else. Even then, don't present all of it in one breathless rush. A more effective way is to work in part of the idea casually, in the middle of a conversation, rather than announcing, "I have a great idea and I want your opinion."

Release more details only if you get a positive reaction. Then listen for feedback. Write it all down. Then review it again and again. If the idea isn't big enough to demand your total effort, if it doesn't dominate most of your waking hours, then it may not be worth pursuing. It may be simply a part-time idea. Remember, your investment hasn't been wasted. But, like any true fisherman, you hope for a bigger one next time.

• • • • • • • • • • • • • • • • • • • •

*There's nothing convenient
about a new idea.
Ideas surface in your brain like
a baby's smile. They are purely
beautiful but for only an instant.
Have the camera ready—
take the baby's picture.*

• • • • • • • • • • • • • • • • • • • •

To be sure, not every idea is going to rank with the electric light bulb. A company can speed along on silken wings when it is fueled by small, innovative ideas that enhance performance or efficiency. Any idea is a valuable one if it increases business, improves customer relations or raises employee morale.

At Kwik Kopy we instituted a program called Bud Bucks. Actually, we kind of stumbled into it, which is as good a way as any. The original Bud Bucks were S&H green stamps. Back in our early days, we ran into a problem that exists with most companies today and will be with us always. This is the thorny matter of getting paid promptly.

It was easy for a franchise owner to put Kwik Kopy last. Naturally, we feel we should come first. You try to find that happy ground in between, but the issue can get frosty. When you have a concern for your owners, you have a tendency to let them slide. When about 82 percent of your income is from franchise royalties, and you rely on that percentage, you simply must collect it or you can't stay in business.

So twenty years ago, just getting up steam in the franchising field, we were confronted with this problem of people paying their royalties when it was convenient. We had to do something. I can remember standing at the door and looking down the street for the mailman, hoping for a check to pay the utility bills. It was that tight.

An idea came to me. I went to the showroom for S&H Green Stamps and picked up an armload of catalogues. Then I sent a catalog with a letter to each of the wives of the franchise owners, along with a thousand green stamps. The letter explained that every time the owner paid his royalty on time, the center would receive a gift of green stamps, one for every dollar of royalty. As you can imagine,

*Ideas are the food, water
and life's blood of the
entrepreneur.*

that move didn't make me immensely popular among the husbands. However, there was an immediate response. I came to work on a Monday morning and found an envelope slipped under the door. Each day there were more. One owner wrote me a three-page letter, chewing me out because he had to spend an entire weekend bringing his books up to date. Yet, enclosed was a check, and the last paragraph said to make sure that his wife received those blankety-blank stamps.

I knew then that this idea was a good one.

Eventually, green stamps faded away. To replace them, we gave a cash discount for on-time payments. Then it occurred to me that if it worked before, it could work again. We simply had to be a little more innovative. So we introduced Bud Bucks (we all enjoy having babies named after us and I modestly accepted the honor). The owners not only earned them for paying their franchise service fee on time, they also received them for writing articles for our company magazine, the *Kwik Kopy Kids*, for attending seminars, or sending in advertising pieces we distribute to other centers. Bud Bucks can be redeemed at the company store, with a slight string attached. This is not a mail order business. The only way to redeem them is to come to the campus for a seminar and shop in person.

This incentive is part of an overall plan, but it was dumb luck that it worked out so much better than we expected. We had to more than double the size of the company store to accommodate the traffic.

The program had a ripple effect, it attracted owners to campus seminars and it strengthened the relationship between the corporation and the franchise owners. You have to give them a mighty good reason to write out a check to you every month. We must offer a multitude of advantages

• •

Money can't save a failure.
Money generally isn't the cause
of a failure. It's symptomatic.
Don't ask the banker, the lawyer
or your college professor. Go to
an entrepreneur and ask him, or
her, to look at your situation. In
all probability, that person was
in the same predicament
sometime in the past.

• •

to keep our people happy. You can't hold them by contract alone.

Ideas are the food, water and life's blood of the entrepreneur, a word that appears with some regularity in these pages. For over half a century now I have been an entrepreneur, and for most of those years I didn't know it. The label has become popular and even respectable over the past few years. It is perceived in a much different way than it once was. Entrepreneurs used to be described as promoters or even hustlers, which put us a half-step above carnival barkers and a full step behind used car salesmen.

I remember Mr. Philpot from my childhood, a Southern gentleman from Georgia who had a chauffeur-driven Cadillac. His son, about my age, had an allowance close to my father's salary. Mr. Philpot's claim to fame was found through the smokestack—you know, the kind of extended chimney that factories used to belch out soot, which eventually finds its way into every nook and cranny in town.

In a sense, Mr. Philpot was a traveling salesman, and what he sold was one of the earliest and crudest versions of what we now call "pollution control," or even "environmental protection." Not that he actually had those conditions in mind.

There was nothing complicated about his technique, and it worked quite well. First, Mr. Philpot met with factory owners or their general managers. He would describe in ominous terms the dangers of a smokestack. He would tell them that one day these towers of danger could crumble by their own weight, cause the roof to collapse and wreck costly equipment. They might even kill a few poor, unsuspecting souls. The man from Georgia sure could sell, and the cost-conscious, penny-pinching Yankees bought it. After all, who could stand the cost

• • • • • • • • • • • • • • • • • • • •

*An entrepreneur sees
what hasn't happened yet
and is willing to bet his or
her last dime to enable the
rest of us to see it too.
This takes courage
and brains.*

• • • • • • • • • • • • • • • • • • • •

of replacing a towering smokestack?

He called on every factory in town. He usually closed the sale with a no-cost inspection. A specialist (whatever that is) would lower himself down the stack, chip away at the bricks until a few loosened enough to be removed and taken as trophies to management. Yes, it was a grave meeting where everyone looked at the bricks and in unison their heads shook until the boss stopped shaking and started nodding. The cost was high, but the consequences could be so much worse. So, the crew went to work inside the brick chimney, where no one in management really cared to inspect. A few weeks later, the job would be complete, and Mr. Philpot wound up with a nice check in his hand.

However, before he left town, someone in Providence, Rhode Island, must have asked the question, "Why are all our smokestacks in such bad shape at the same time?" When people got to thinking about it, they decided to act. A brave soul volunteered to go down a few of the black holes and inspect whatever work had been done. The answer wasn't exactly in Mr. Philpot's favor.

The business leaders were so outraged they yanked that elderly Southerner out of the backseat of his Cadillac and put him in a jail cell. He was charged, tried, found guilty and sent to prison.

I honestly don't know whether Mr. Philpot was guilty of fraud or not. I do know he was close to legally blind and couldn't have found his way home without help, which gained him no sympathy in Providence. It may well be that he was simply ahead of his time. Branded as a promoter or con artist, he wound up behind bars. Fifty years later, he might have been perceived as an "entrepreneur" and given a banquet.

• •

If you work it right,

everything in life is a

learning experience.

These are some of mine.

No matter how closely I

read them, I find no

formulas or recipes for

instant success.

• • • • • • • • • • • • • • • • • • • •

Perceptions do change. Most entrepreneurs whom I have known are honest, hard-working men and women who have a spark others are missing. They love with a passion what they are doing, even more so than the wealth they may be accumulating. They have a special kind of "vision with substance." An entrepreneur sees what hasn't happened yet and is willing to bet his or her last dime to enable the rest of us to see it too. This takes courage and brains.

If you are wondering what makes this kind of person tick, I'll tell you two places not to look and the one place where you will find the truth.

WHERE NOT TO LOOK

The Print Media—Newspapers and magazines rarely provide a full picture of the entrepreneur in action. This isn't sour grapes on my part; I have been treated far more kindly than most. However, the writer or reporter is trained to get the facts and interpret them in an interesting way to capture and hold your attention. If it is a choice between cold facts or colorful speculation, you and I both know which will survive in print. Be honest. Would you read a magazine or newspaper story if it wasn't made easy and provocative to read? Fiction is fun.

Books Written by an Honored Member of Academia—I refer, of course, to those intellectuals (or close to it) who spend most of their lives in education and do not really understand the first practical principle of building a business. From the viewpoint of the isolated scholar, an entrepreneur is a person with an idea and lots of enthusiasm—sometimes interpreted as loud and boasting. It is true that most entrepreneurs have little patience with the crunching

• • • • • • • • • • • • • • • • • • •

Get off your assets and go
ask the man or woman
who is in the process of
turning an idea into
the reality of an
honest-to-goodness
business.
You will get real answers.

• • • • • • • • • • • • • • • • • • •

of numbers, but you can be sure they understand the bottom line and the major methods of determining it. They are anything but mindless idiots in a mad rush for riches.

WHERE TO LOOK

How to Find Out for Yourself—Get off your assets and go ask the man or woman who is in the process of turning an idea into the reality of an honest-to-goodness business. You will get real answers. You may not agree with them and may not understand them. There is an outside chance you never will.

With financial assistance from my father and mother I bought my first second-hand printing press before I was twelve. It was a hand-operated job that today would be at home in any health and fitness center. It surely built the muscles in my right arm and shoulder. By the time I entered the printing class at Hugh B. Bain Junior High School in Cranston, *The Family Press*, the name of my newspaper, was a hustling enterprise with two presses, one of them powered by an electric motor.

If you work it right, everything in life is a learning experience. These are some of mine. No matter how closely I read them, I find no formulas or recipes for instant success. Pick and choose among the ideas I have tried and the mistakes I have made to find the ones that may benefit you.

Of course, we would all be successful if we followed the advice we give to others.

Chapter

7

The
Turnaround

George Allen…came out of retirement to coach a college football team at Long Beach State. Two months before his death, they celebrated their first winning season in years.

A friend of mine tells a story about the late football coach, George Allen, one of the great motivators of his time. Allen was invited to be the speaker at a convention of Chrysler dealers at a time when the company was in shambles. They were close to bankruptcy and were negotiating a $2 billion loan from the government.

Allen believed in motivation so strongly that, at the age of seventy-two, he came out of retirement to coach a college football team at Long Beach State. Two months before his death, they celebrated their first winning season in years.

Allen faced problems of another kind as he prepared to address the Chrysler dealers. He wasn't familiar with the car business. He was unsure what to tell these men who saw dealerships closing all around them. The company stock was trading below $3.

He wanted to draw on his experiences in football to give his audience some lesson that might apply to the automobile industry. He knew they would be hoping for an insight or an idea that might be adapted as a sales tactic.

On the morning of his talk, Coach Allen found his

• • • • • • • • • • • • • • • • • • •

*Allen also described how
he kept a "talk chart," an
expression no one
understood. He explained:
"A talk chart helps me
keep in touch with the
people around me."*

• • • • • • • • • • • • • • • • • • •

The Turnaround

theme. He looked out into his audience, representing the fifty or sixty surviving Chrysler outlets across the country (out of a high of nearly two hundred) and he said:

"This is great! You have gotten rid of all the quitters and front runners and you are down to just the winners. The people in this room are the pros, the ones who won't fold. These are the people you can count on, the ones who didn't get in because the car business looked like a way to make a quick buck. You can't help but succeed now. You're down to the people who will stick it out and turn things around."

Then he told a story about his first coaching job in 1948, at tiny Morningside College in Iowa. "That year I kept putting up notices and writing letters and begging everybody to come out for football. We wound up with a hundred players, and we didn't have uniforms for all of them. Some came out in shorts, with no pads. I put them on two-a-day practices for three straight weeks and the players started dropping out, quitting. Soon I had plenty of uniforms to go around.

"Then the number shrank to fifty, and then forty. I began to worry that we wouldn't have enough players to open the season. We got down to twenty-seven. I had only five substitutes in case of injury. To make matters worse, we played an eleven-game schedule, unusual for those days.

"Well, we lost only three of those games. The reason was simple: We had the cream of the crop. These were the guys who should have been out there in the first place, who wanted to play. And they were in great condition. They were in shape."

Allen also described how he kept a "talk chart," an

• • • • • • • • • • • • • • • • • • • •

*Lack of money is not the
cause of a business failure.
The lack of money is
symptomatic of business
failure.*

• • • • • • • • • • • • • • • • • • • •

expression no one understood. He explained: "A talk chart helps me keep in touch with the people around me. It shows me when I last talked to players on the team, or in the office, even in some of the so-called fringe jobs. Everybody's name is on there. If I didn't consult the chart, I might find that six weeks would go by, and I hadn't talked with one of our starting tackles or a wide receiver, or the equipment manager, the security man or the team dentist.

"You get so busy and preoccupied with other problems, you don't realize how easy it is to lose touch. By keeping a chart, I made it a point to call them in. It is a way to let them know you are interested and concerned...of finding out what they think, what their problems are. I taped the chart to one of those desk shelves that pull out. Each time I talked with someone, I wrote down the date and hour by his name. It was a small thought, but it is a way of pulling together and staying together."

Companies move in many ways, some small, some large. Allen did what a gifted motivator does: he identified the problem, reduced it to a theme, and surrounded it with hope and an example that worked.

I'm not naive. That $2 billion federal loan kept Chrysler afloat. But lack of money alone didn't take the company to the brink of failing, and money didn't guarantee that it could stage a comeback.

Lack of money is *not* the cause of a business failure. The lack of money is symptomatic of business failure. It is only one of the many symptoms of a failing business.

There are many reasons why a business dies, and until those reasons are addressed and corrective measures are implemented, there can be no hope for a return to a healthy enterprise. Keep these two rules in mind:

• • • • • • • • • • • • • • • • • • •

*Good employees won't
work for bad bosses—not
for long. I've never seen
a happy shop
with a bad boss.*

• • • • • • • • • • • • • • • • • • •

1. Cutting quality to save money is like stopping the clock to save time. Eliminate waste. Cut fat, not quality.

2. Trying to collect small debts when there are not enough dollars to go around is like trying to pick fruit from a drought-stricken garden.

When a business has slipped past the point of having enough cash to meet obligations, it enters the zone of diminishing liquid assets. When this happens there is only one way back to health, and it isn't easy.

First, diagnose the effects and change them from negative to positive. The dry plant that doesn't produce needs water. The business that is in trouble needs dollars. BUT—and it's a mighty big "but"—the dollars in themselves are not enough to make a lasting change.

Assume that the bank approves a substantial loan and, for the time being, a feeling of euphoria prevails. The boss smiles at most of his problems and the employees feel pretty mellow about things. Then the money runs out, bill collectors start calling again and the effect of it all produces a series of negative occurrences. When the law of cause and effect is disturbed, all kinds of consequences are generated.

Smiles turn to frowns. Small situations escalate into major problems. The boss, driven by money worries, explodes and vents his frustration at the least excuse. Employees are verbally abused during work hours. You find yourself leaning on the horn in traffic. And families suffer at the dinner table.

Good employees won't work for bad bosses, not for long. I've never seen a happy shop with a bad boss. And so it goes. The sun shines for a few days and the greenery reappears. This is nature. This is business.

All of which brings us to the next point: Bringing a

• •

Resign from
all your worries.
When you can mentally
do this, good things have a
way of working for you.

• • • • • • • • • • • • • • • • • • • •

company back to robust health sounds noble and heroic. It is. However, an even bigger problem lurks in the garden, called weeds. They can be found in the office culture, too. The top man has to be responsible for weed control.

The road back must be the responsibility of someone other than the survivors. That is where the rub comes. Who should that someone be?

A few years ago, Kwik Kopy initiated a program called Fresh Start. It was a fine idea with one exception. We left it up to the franchise owners, including those struggling to carry out our suggestions. Some did. Others failed in varying degrees.

This inconsistency led to a revised program called Fresh Start II. This time we would take an active and ongoing position until one of three things happened:

1. The owner adopted the program and continued.

2. The owner sold out.

3. We closed the center.

Admittedly, we walk a tightrope in an approach so paternal, or even dictatorial. It must be planned with great care and thoughtfulness. However, I believe it can be adapted by a business of any size. It is worth a try.

These are the fundamentals:

FRESH START II

An Outline

I. A center is identified as a candidate and the owner agrees to participate subject to a contractual agreement.

II. The agreement should cover the following:

• • • • • • • • • • • • • • • • • • • •

*Admittedly, we walk a
tightrope in an approach
so paternal, or even
dictatorial. It must be
planned with great care
and thoughtfulness.*

• • • • • • • • • • • • • • • • • • • •

A. Kwik Kopy Corporation will loan money on an ongoing basis for a period of time; Kwik Kopy Corporation can withdraw from the program by discontinuing financial support at any time without a stated reason.

B. The owner agrees to draw a salary and no other compensation without written approval from the corporation.

C. All necessary cash expenditure controls are in place, and a priority payment list is agreed upon by both parties. The first three each month are: payroll, taxes and the corporation.

D. The owner agrees to a marketing plan which includes but is not limited to the following:

  1. A specified number of sales calls to new prospects each week.

  2. A direct mail program.

  3. Control of purchasing, labor and all other costs.

This basic outline fits almost any situation. In place of Kwik Kopy, insert your own franchisor or parent company, or any lending source, family, friends or a sympathetic banker (if that isn't a contradiction in terms.) To work, the agreement must be strict; it must be in writing and it must be kept. Coming from behind, or starting over, is seldom easy. But it is far preferable to the alternative, which is not to try. Consider this: What do you do next when you want to quit?

My advice is, go ahead and quit...but in mind only. Mentally throw up your hands and walk away. Give that remarkable mind of yours some worry-free time and space. Tell yourself that it's over and you have lost. Lost every-

• • • • • • • • • • • • • • • • • • •

Winning is a habit.

Unfortunately, so is losing.

• • • • • • • • • • • • • • • • • • •

thing. There is nothing left to fight for, nothing to salvage. Resign from all your worries. When you can mentally do this, good things have a way of working for you.

Everyone's natural desire is to avoid losing. Do you know the definition of a loser? Take your choice. A loser is the kind of person who plays the piano in a marching band. A loser is someone who saves up all his life for a cemetery plot and gets buried at sea. A loser goes to the gourmet shelf in his supermarket looking for Philadelphia Cream Cheese.

You get the idea. The world has been and always will be made up of three kinds of people—winners, losers and the great majority who fall somewhere in-between. The in-betweeners sometimes know they are, but rarely know why. Nor do they have a sense of where they are headed.

It makes good sense to me that when you associate with winners, you have a better chance to be a winner. The same rule applies to losers. We all have a tendency to take on the shading of the people with whom we associate. We adopt their ways, their attitudes, even their habits. Winning is a habit. Unfortunately, so is losing.

I can tell you from personal experience, it hurts to lose. It is a miserable, rotten, useless feeling. You alternate between resentment and embarrassment, with flashes of pure, white-hot anger. Losing is like swimming below the surface in a sewer and being afraid to come up for air. All you want is to be alone, to hurt alone, to enjoy your self-pity.

Finally, the healing process swings into action—if you allow it. Your mind scrambles for thoughts to soften the memory of defeat. The words that have helped me as much as any are these:

● ● ● ● ● ● ● ● ● ● ● ● ● ● ● ● ● ● ●

Become an expert in your field. Know more about your business than your competitors and certainly know more than your customers.

● ● ● ● ● ● ● ● ● ● ● ● ● ● ● ● ● ● ●

A failure can stop me.
But it can't keep me from trying again.

The population of Houston was about 1.2 million in 1973 when I ran for mayor and lost. To me, it seemed as if 2.4 million eyes saw me as a loser. I quit going out for lunch because I just knew that everyone in the room mentally pointed me out as the jerk who lost the mayor's race.

Maudlin self-pity is stupid. But at the time, it was the only way I could deal with what I considered a humiliating reversal. I continued to think that way until a friend, a real political pro, said to me, "Why worry about what others think? Judging by the number of votes you got, no one knows who you are anyway." Whereupon I quickly went back to eating in public.

From that defeat, I filed away two important lessons:

1. *Make a total commitment to your goal.* I hadn't been willing to make the sacrifices necessary to win the election. The candidate who won had lost a previous bid for the mayor's job two years earlier, but that didn't stop him. Between elections he attended hundreds of public functions and built a campaign team of dedicated followers who believed as he did, that he was the best man for the job. I campaigned for seven months, against his twenty-four.

2. *Always know what you are selling.* No matter what your field or profession, you are in reality a salesman. No matter what product you think you sell, cars or insurance or plumbing supplies, we all sell the same product. I once met a young man who told me he sold houses. I taunted him by asking, "And what do houses buy?"

"No," he said, grinning at my thickness, "I sell houses, places where people live."

• • • • • • • • • • • • • • • • • • •

Readiness makes for opportunity. Opportunity often comes by accident. Readiness never does.

—Sam Rayburn

• • • • • • • • • • • • • • • • • • •

And I repeated my question until finally in exasperation he said, "What's your point? Houses don't buy anything. People buy houses."

Bingo! "You're right," I said. "People buy houses. People buy cars. You can't sell others until you know how to sell yourself." Charles Schwab, one of America's all-time great negotiators, used to say we are all salesmen every day of our lives—selling ideas, plans, and enthusiasms to all we come in contact with.

The man who sells life insurance feels he is really in the business of protecting families or helping people build a secure future.

Plumbing supplies are nothing more than costly inventory until people buy them.

If selling ourselves is the universal experience, there is a practical way to begin. Become an expert in your field. Know more about your business than your competitors and certainly know more than your customers. Be prepared, be ready. The late Sam Rayburn, the longtime Speaker of the House from Texas, once said: "Readiness makes for opportunity. Opportunity often comes by accident. Readiness never does."

Another cautionary note—don't oversell. Once you have shaken off those Elmer Fudd feelings of meekness, don't be the vacuum cleaner salesman who hopes no one is home—be sure you don't create a monster.

When I first taught the Dale Carnegie course and tasted some success, I fell into the same trap as many other instructors. You get pumped up. Move over, world, I'm here. And you take credit for something that has nothing to do with you. It is like a lounge singer who belts out one of the classics, maybe "Stardust," and the crowd applauds.

• • • • • • • • • • • • • • • • • • • •

If selling ourselves is the
universal experience,
there is a practical way
to begin. Become an
expert in your field.

• • • • • • • • • • • • • • • • • • • •

The applause is for the writer, Hoagy Carmichael, or the artist who recorded it, but that doesn't prevent the lounge singer from interrupting himself to say, "Thank you, thank you."

When my sponsor at Carnegie, Jim Trivette, gave me a chance to teach, he attached a condition. He sent me to the city of Corpus Christi and said, "If you can sell a class, you can teach it." I wanted to teach so badly, I went everywhere to sign up potential students. A woman who managed a beauty parlor answered one of our ads, and I called on her. She was with a customer when I walked in. "Sit over there," she pointed, "and I'll be right with you."

I never imagined myself sitting in a beauty parlor, but there I was, sitting next to a lady whose head was under a hair dryer. Neither of us was doing anything, so I swung into my sales pitch. She looked at me incredulously, but appeared on the first night and signed up for the course. On graduation night, she said, "Bud, you may not remember, but we met at a beauty parlor. The reason I was there, I was getting my hair fixed because I intended to commit suicide. My husband and I had just gone broke with a small business we owned. He was an alcoholic. I didn't think I had any reason to live. I wanted to look good when I killed myself."

I have no way of knowing how serious her intentions were. However, the implications of her story inflated my ego beyond my control. The effect on me was devastating. I thought I was Saint Bud. Then one night Jim Trivette said, "When are you going to start teaching the Dale Carnegie course?" I said, "What do you mean, I've been teaching it for the past two years."

He said, "No, you've been teaching the Bud Hadfield course." I had to make a deep self-assessment. A person

• • • • • • • • • • • • • • • • • •

Be a clipper…Which of my friends has a happening in his or her life? When I find a complimentary item, I cut it out and mail it to him with a brief congratulatory note the SAME DAY.

• • • • • • • • • • • • • • • • • •

with a large ego seldom admits to it. He may laugh or joke, but he doesn't believe he really has one. He just thinks he's great. My mental fuse box had to be rewired. It was one of the most significant lessons I ever learned: don't take credit for what someone else did better than you ever could.

Perhaps this is where a distinction needs to be made. There are two kinds of turnaround, one business and one personal. At times they overlap. In either case, here are seven tried and tested, effective human relation principles that will help you influence others by giving them something they don't expect—something extra.

1. *Remember Birthdays.* Every year I send out several hundred birthday and anniversary cards to friends, associates and customers. The results are amazing. In my files are letters from people all across the social and business strata, those who create wealth and those who dispose of waste. Each in his or her own way wrote to express thanks for my having remembered their birthday.

You will learn, as I did, that few people outside of one's immediate family ever remember birthdays.

2. *Be a Clipper.* My day begins at three-thirty in the morning. Each day I try to read our local papers, trade journals, service club bulletins, church bulletins and civic club newsletters with one idea in mind—which of my friends has a happening in his or her life?

When I find a complimentary item, I cut it out and mail it to him with a brief congratulatory note the SAME DAY. (The sportscaster Harry Wismer went through life like a truck with a loudspeaker on it, greeting anyone who crossed his path with one word: "Congratulations." He did so on the theory that the word was harmless and many people routinely experience nice things. Not surprisingly,

• • • • • • • • • • • • • • • • • • •

*Pick up the phone
right now, or after you
finish this page and
place a call to some person
you really like but haven't
talked with lately.*

• • • • • • • • • • • • • • • • • • •

many replied, "How did you know?"

3. *Make the "Focused" Phone Call.* Sam Clark was a school dropout at the age of ten. Poverty forced him out of school to help support his family. Starting out as a helper in a machine shop, he gradually worked his way up the ladder. Sam rose to the position of executive vice president of the Keystone Valve Corporation and became widely sought as a speaker at sales conventions across the nation.

How did he achieve this? Did he know more about valves than anybody else? Perhaps. But I like to believe he knew more about people.

Because of his demanding schedule, he used his telephone as an instrument of good will. He excelled in what I call the "focused" phone call. For example, when Sam called my number he always took the time to ask about the events in my life, my family, my business, my activities. A conversation with Sam made the whole day brighter. He was sincerely interested in me and what I had to say.

Be like Sam and make the "focused" phone call. Focus on the person at the other end of the line. Pick up the phone right now, or after you finish this page and place a call to some person you really like but haven't talked with lately. Ask about their personal lives. Be interested in what they say. At least two things will happen: First, the person you call will be pleasantly impressed, and second, you will get the kind of warm glow inside that money simply can't buy.

4. *Tell Friends They Are Special.* Build a file, if only in your head, of the hobbies, sports or other interests that are important to your friends and associates. Take any opportunity to let them know you are thinking about them. Send them a newspaper article, an advertisement, a book or even a souvenir that relates to their interest. This is one

• • • • • • • • • • • • • • • • • •

When I speak, less than
three percent of the
married men in my
audiences can answer
"yes"
to this question:
Have you surprised
your wife in the last
six months by giving her
a dozen roses?

• • • • • • • • • • • • • • • • • •

of the best ways I know to never forget a friend, nor to let them forget you.

5. *Nurture Your Family.* When I speak, less than 3 percent of the married men in my audiences can answer yes to this question: Have you surprised your wife in the last six months by giving her a dozen roses? And yet a doctor friend of mine told me how roses actually changed the course of the events in his life and the lives of his family.

"For a couple of years," he began, "my wife and I had been on the outs. In fact, we would have filed for divorce had it not been for our six-year-old son. Our family life had so degenerated that I spent as much time as possible away from home. My wife had adopted a cold, 'I couldn't care less' attitude. At least, it seemed so to me.

"A close friend and I were discussing the problem when he asked me the same question I just asked you. He felt that flowers were a way of showing appreciation and a bouquet can express, in thought, what we never seem capable of saying in words. The message struck a nerve and that night, on the way home, I stopped at the florist and made a purchase.

"As I drove into the driveway, my courage seemed to leave me and I wondered how I could get rid of the flowers without her knowing. Finally, it just seemed easier to take them in the house. Entering the back door that opens to the kitchen, I noticed my wife bent over the sink peeling potatoes for dinner. It was terribly awkward, but I managed to place the flowers on the drainboard. She didn't look up as I said, 'Here's some flowers. They're for…well…because you try to make this house livable.' "

Can you imagine those fumbling words as a compliment? The results seemed disastrous. "She didn't even look

*In today's rush and
impersonal business
climate, it is unusual
to find someone
doing more than what
they were expected to do.
How about you?*

up," the doctor went on. "She just kept right on peeling potatoes. I went into the living room and sat back in my easy chair, determined to forget the whole thing by reading the paper.

"In a few minutes our young son came running through the living room and into the kitchen. I could hear through the swinging door that leads into the kitchen as he asked, 'Mom, where did the flowers come from?'

" 'Your daddy brought them to us,' she said. 'Why?' he asked.

"There was what seemed a long pause and then in a strange, muffled voice I heard my wife say, 'I guess it's because he loves us.'

"Well, the next thing I knew, my young son had run back into the room and with a push, knocked the evening paper from my hand. He wrapped his little arms around my legs, looked me squarely in the eye and with tears streaming down his cheeks he blurted out, 'We love you, too, Dad.'

" 'But why are you crying?' I asked.

"He said, 'I guess because Mom is crying.'

"That night, after our son had gone to bed, I put my arms around my wife and held her close. At last, I realized how hungry she had been for some kind of appreciation, affection or just plain recognition. That's when our lives started to change. Today we are happier than ever before. Our son has grown and is married to a wonderful girl. Years ago, he was our reason for staying together. Now our reason is our love and appreciation of each other." It began with a dozen roses.

6. *Use the Third Man Theme.* Recently, when I tried to tell someone how much I admired him, he interrupted me

• • • • • • • • • • • • • • • • • •

Give them something
unexpected,
something extra.
The results may
surprise you.

• • • • • • • • • • • • • • • • • •

with a broad smile and a pat on the shoulder. "Bud, don't tell me," he said. "Tell someone else. When it gets back to me, and I know it will, I'll appreciate it even more."

Write yourself a reminder to pay compliments about those not in your presence. Do it for a week...and another week...and stay with it until you form the habit of the Third Man Theme.

7. Waste Not, Want Not. In my early days as a printer, I bought an oversupply of air mail envelopes. Even my customers couldn't buy enough to make any appreciable dent in the stock. One of the men in the shop had an idea that seemed worth trying. He suggested giving them away by including some with every order for plain envelopes. We tried it. The results were astonishing; our business soared. In less than a year we were printing more envelopes in a single week than we had printed in the busiest month of the previous year.

What happened? What caused our sales to jump? There were several reasons, but in talking with our customers, one factor surfaced more than any other. Those few air mail envelopes were something extra; they were more than the customer believed was part of the bargain.

In today's rush and impersonal business climate, it is unusual to find someone doing more than they were expected to do. How about you? What can you give your family, friends and associates? Give them something unexpected, something extra. The results may surprise you.

Chapter

8

BEWARE—
The Final Chapter

• • • • • • • • • • • • • • • • • • •

"He learned to say hello
when it was time to say
good-bye."

• • • • • • • • • • • • • • • • • • •

It was once said of a difficult actor, who mellowed and turned friendly in the twilight of his career: "He learned to say hello when it was time to say good-bye."

With a good many mixed feelings, I want to address in these pages that moment when the founder of a company, or anyone in a position of authority, needs to think about saying good-bye.

You have been around for fifteen or twenty years, perhaps longer, and you discover a moment not unlike the hush at the ballpark just before the playing of "The Star Spangled Banner." It is that added emotional impact when the final moment is in sight, just before departing...and you're not quite ready for it. The last few words before the first few tears. The physical parting followed by a mental process we call memory.

Experience teaches us that we remember much less than we forget. Do you remember your "golden" schooldays? Let's face it. Unless you have the heart of a statue, you are going to be engulfed by feelings of nostalgia. We try to tough it out, taking the position that nostalgia ought to go back where it came from. In reality, penny candy

• • • • • • • • • • • • • • • • • • • •

Initial enthusiasm has a way of rolling over the mistakes of a fresh start.

• • • • • • • • • • • • • • • • • • • •

rotted your teeth, the ice you swiped from the back of the truck was filthy, and while it was fun to ride a train, you usually wound up with a cinder in your eye.

Why am I sharing these somewhat sentimental feelings with you? Do we, I wonder, go our different ways with the last volley by a writer who delivers a maudlin piece of worldly luggage, or is there just one more point I must make? If you have read this entire book, then I feel I owe you something. You are entitled to the most compelling lesson I have learned in the business of how to succeed in business.

This is exactly why I have entitled these final pages, "BEWARE—the Final Chapter." It might very well help you to make the final chapter in your own career more than you hoped for. It might save you from the empty days and plodding weeks and wasted years of succeeding without happiness. What I am about to tell you could be your new beginning, right now, starting with this very moment in time. Immediately!

Let me begin with a true story about my friend Bill, who did everything right—that is, right up to the last chapter, to that one irreversible decision. It was a big one and a bad one. Even worse, a plaintive ending to a brilliant career.

It started about a quarter century ago when Bill conceived an idea to expand his business by franchising across the country. He successfully managed his business for many years, and now he was straining at the leash to take on the most significant challenge of his life.

Initial enthusiasm has a way of rolling over the mistakes of a fresh start. In Bill's case, he did just about everything right the first time around. The training program was

BUD'S BUSINESS DOZEN **#12**

Success comes to
the man or woman
who gives more
than receives.

the distillation of his many years in business. In three weeks, a former accountant, a salesman, and a trucker learned enough about the business to open their own and immediately compete in the marketplace. The franchisor and his franchisees worked in concert as they mutually grew and prospered.

They learned the vital lessons of cash management, business planning, cost efficient advertising, personnel policies and even the not-so-pleasant legal issues that seem to invade every commercial enterprise. Almost everyone involved achieved financial success.

The company grew at a breathtaking pace. One of the paramount advantages of franchising is the franchisor expands under the OPM principle: Other People's Money. In Bill's case, his locations multiplied so fast it became necessary to raise additional capital by taking the company public. First, a limited offering was made. The stock appeared on the over-the-counter listings. Not much later, they moved into a faster league, the American Stock Exchange, and he used the money to build at a faster rate. Almost overnight, my friend became a multimillionaire.

But that is not the end of the story. It is the beginning of the end of the story.

Somewhere along the way, Bill, the company founder, got the idea that the game had changed and he was in over his head. He told himself that the responsibilities of running a large corporation were out of his range of management expertise. I remember so clearly the day we talked on the phone about his bringing in a head-hunter to find a qualified executive to act as president, who would later be elevated to the position of chief executive officer.

• •

The shadow of a single
man will determine
the destiny of an
entire business.
—*Ralph Waldo Emerson*

• • • • • • • • • • • • • • • • • • • •

I listened to this news with disbelief and a sense of foreboding. "Why, Bill?" I asked.

"You may not know it, Bud," he said, "but I never went to college. All I have is a high school diploma."

"So what?" I countered. "I never even graduated from high school!"

I feel I was more saddened than he was by the course he had chosen to take. He said he felt he needed a professional to run the business. I was chagrined. "Bill," I argued, "you built the business. Nobody knows it like you do." His owners adored him. In truth, he had a better relationship with most of his than I did with mine. He was this kind of person: He kept a file on his Rolodex and before he called anyone he always reviewed their card, because he wanted to be right. He wanted to know their wife's name, if they still had their dog. A good man.

However, he wasn't listening. He was sending, not receiving. His mind was made up and the beginning-of-the-end scenario had been put in motion.

It started with the new CEO replacing key staff members who had been loyal to Bill for years with his own people. In time the turnover was complete and the next phase was put into operation. Bill was eased out of the mainstream of decision making and, along with it, stripped of any real authority. He was isolated. Next came the confrontation with the board of directors, which now consisted of people who felt no obligation to the founder of the company. The new CEO easily out-talked him. He knew what was going on and Bill didn't. He was cut off from any meaningful information. He lost control of the business. The board made it official and shoved him out the back door. I heard that he walked away a wealthy man with ben-

• • • • • • • • • • • • • • • • • • •

BEWARE!
Information is power.
You can delegate
authority and still
maintain control.
You cannot—
I said, CANNOT—
delegate your
responsibility with any
valid hope of
still running the business.

• • • • • • • • • • • • • • • • • • •

efits worth millions of dollars. But I can assure you, he did not walk away a happy man.

BEWARE! Information is power. You can delegate authority and still maintain control. You cannot—I said, CANNOT—delegate your responsibility with any valid hope of still running the business.

"So," you ask, "what is the difference between authority and responsibility?"

Authority means that I freely give you permission to carry out certain actions under my control. Responsibility is bottom line; the final say-so. Give up the ultimate actions to another and inevitably, over time, you give up your business as well.

BEWARE! Do you know what you are? Do you really know? Are you an entrepreneur? Or are you a promoter? Again, is there a difference? Twenty-five years ago, you never heard the word *entrepreneur*. If you considered yourself a person of ideas, you were a promoter, and the name had a less than savory image.

In case you feel any confusion, let me offer my definitions. The entrepreneur is a special breed. He or she is a person with a gift of vision. The entrepreneur sees what others never envision. Usually, it is a new idea that becomes a business venture. So far, so good. But there's more.

The genuine entrepreneur becomes so dedicated to a concept that he or she is oblivious to just about everything else. An entrepreneur sees each problem as an opportunity, and then, from what source no one knows, comes the answer and the excitement stirs. All hell breaks loose and all systems are go. It becomes a game. Not a contest, a game. All the players win, not just the principal character.

Ralph Waldo Emerson defined it pretty well when he

• • • • • • • • • • • • • • • • • • • •

Don't sell yourself short!

• • • • • • • • • • • • • • • • • • • •

said, "The shadow of a single man will determine the destiny of an entire business." Your place in the sun must be positioned always so that you cast the biggest shadow of all.

But, what about the label "promoter"?

In many ways, the two are much alike. There are, however, certain sharp distinctions. Let's take a look:

A promoter promotes. And once the plan has been brought to fruition, the promoter sells out and is on his way to greener pastures. Generally, it's the promoter who wins. Only the promoter. In many instances, the promoter promotes what another person dreamed up in the first place. To capture a good idea and do nothing about it, in my opinion, is worse than never having an idea at all. And that brings us to our next point.

BEWARE! Don't sell yourself short because you wrongly believe it is "only my idea." It wasn't your idea to begin with; it came to you from some elusive corner of the cosmos, if not a dark recess of the mind. It is a gift that no one else can claim. Some people sing beautifully without a solitary lesson. Others paint. Still others write, build bridges, do heart transplants. When I write, I turn my mind over to an influence I don't understand. I just write the words as they come to me. If you have the gift of new ideas, you can do one of three things:

1. Lack the courage to do something, anything, about your idea, and it goes away and surfaces through another person.

2. Simply talk about an idea until it is picked up and acted upon by someone more decisive, possibly a promoter.

3. You are compelled to go for it—and you make things happen. Others benefit from you and your idea. Because

To me the moral is not to get carried away by people with zippy words.

it is yours and you live and die for it, you become the principal player. You either lose the most or gain the most. If your excitement takes on an enlarged dimension and you live as you have never lived before, all the lights are on...If your mental engine powers up and all systems are go...If go you must, in spite of all the reasons to the contrary...then, my friend, you *are* an entrepreneur.

My friend Bill took his wealth and started other businesses. He is still looking, still thinking, still yearning anew. And when he finds the one that won't let go and brings the dream to fruition, who would dare to say that he can't enjoy the full ride, that he has to sell before his time? Getting there is only half the reward.

To me the moral is not to get carried away by people with zippy words. For an entrepreneur, I cannot imagine a fate more painful than seeing your company taken over by a promoter, the type who looks out for Number One, who grabs the money and doesn't suffer the great emotional cost if the franchise holders go down the tubes or the employees lose their jobs. Bill was no promoter. He was a man who spent twenty years working and creating and caring. And then, in one of those inexplicable turns, he lost confidence in himself.

To put the message another way: BEWARE! This plea comes from Sir Winston Churchill, whose gift for language had the power to lift and inspire an entire people. Shortly after the conclusion of World War II, he delivered the commencement address to an English university. After a lengthy introduction, Sir Winston slowly rose to his feet, shuffled to the microphone and delivered his entire speech in only six words: "Never...never...never...never...give up."

It was a real tragedy when my father died at Christmas

• • • • • • • • • • • • • • • • • •

Never...never...never...

never...give up.

—Sir Winston Churchill

• • • • • • • • • • • • • • • • • •

the year I was fifteen. But another memory I have is a different sort of tragedy, and it will forever stick with me. Unfortunately, it happens to literally millions of men and women. It has always been this way. Probably always will.

My father was a postal inspector, and I remember him talking about going into the trucking business one day. He made big plans for it, but he never took the leap. Now why did he want to go into the trucking business? He had no connections in trucking. There may have been a reason, but I never knew what it was. Perhaps he didn't either. He died and his dream died with him.

This happens. How about you? Has it happened? Will it? Does it hurt to think about the possibilities you passed because, for one reason or another, you never got off the mark?

One of my longtime, best friends missed the boat. Right after World War II, Ed Fay was involved in international trade. A fellow representing a foreign company came to him and said, "We're impressed with you and we'd like you to have the distributorship in the southwest for our car."

He told them he didn't have the money to invest, and they said that was no problem, they would finance him. Ed thought about it and still said no. "Cars like that won't sell, Americans don't like little cars." The company was Volkswagen. To this day Ed says, "Every time I see a Volkswagen I get sick." I doubt a day goes by that Ed doesn't get that queasy feeling.

The problem with being given an opportunity is that when you first hear of them, you don't know if they are good or bad. You have to accept risk to find out.

There will be countless reasons along the way to walk

• • • • • • • • • • • • • • • • • • •

You are as young as
your last new idea.
—Bud Hadfield,
1992

• • • • • • • • • • • • • • • • • •

away from your job, your goal, your dream. There is never an excuse good enough unless you *want* to walk away. There is an end to every beginning. That is what life is all about. As you controlled the beginning, so can you control the end. A well-planned exit is as important as a well-planned entry. One day, someday, I will leave Kwik Kopy, but not to the promoters, not to strangers, and only after two things have been accomplished:

1. I have met my obligations to the men and women who helped me at the beginning and along the way—our investors, employees, franchise owners, their employees, and the thousands of customers. Because of them our endeavor in the free enterprise system has been a success.

2. I have settled upon my next challenging idea, the kind of idea that yanks me by the scruff of the neck and insists I do something about it. To give it birth and nurture its growth and watch it become a reality. When that happens I will feel like a kid again. That, my friend, is what it is to be an entrepreneur. To be young again...as young as your next idea.

Ideas are the only currency that can't be devalued, a thought that leads me to this final word of encouragement. Nothing can take the place of hard and purposeful work. Talent will not; nothing is more common than unsuccessful men with talent. Education will not; the world is full of educated derelicts.

If you have ideas and persistence, you can't lose. Success is within your reach. So is wealth, which is a product of being successful. Go for it. Plant the flag. Light the torch. Pump yourself up. You can fill in your own motivational blank. The fact is, something incredible is out there waiting to happen.

Index

Index to Wealth Within Reach: Names And Companies

The author may be reached by writing to:

Bud Hadfield
ICED
P. O. Box 777
One Entrepreneur Way
Cypress, TX 77429

For an additional copy or multiple discounts call

Cypress Publishing

1-888-708-9978

30 minutes from Downtown, 200 years from Houston

The Alamo

Rooms, Specifications, Capacities & Seating Styles:

Sleeping Rooms: 11

Alamo Atrium
- 1,537 (53 x 29)
- 200 - Reception
- 140 - Banquet
- 120 - Theater
- 100 - Classroom
- 54 - Hollow Square
- 48 - U Shape
- 36 - Conference

Classroom I
- 962 sq. ft. (37 x 26)
- 137 - Reception
- 80 - Theater
- 48 - Classroom
- 48 - Banquet
- 30 - Hollow Square
- 26 - U Shape
- 20 - Conference

Classroom II
- 588 sq. ft. (28 x 21)
- 84 - Reception
- 36 - Theater
- 32 - Banquet
- 24 - Classroom
- 24 - Hollow Square
- 20 - U Shape
- 16 - Conference

Conference I
- 260 sq. ft. (20 x 13)
- 20 - Theater
- 16 - Classroom
- 14 - Banquet
- 12 - Hollow Square
- 12 - Conference
- 10 - U Shape

Conference II
- 273 sq. ft. (21 x 13)
- 12 - Conference

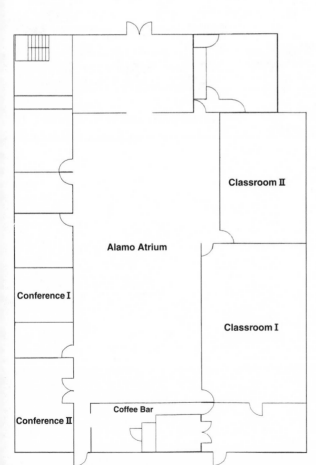

The Alamo

In 1989, using photographs and measured drawings from the Library of Congress, we built our Alamo at Northwest Forest. The weathered stonework matches that of the original, as does the elaborate carving around the doors and windows.

Is there anyone who doesn't know the story of the Alamo?

The Settlement House

Specifications:
>4,648 sq. ft. (83 x 56)

Capacity & Seating Styles:
>500 - Reception
>460 - Theater
>264 - Banquet
>182 - Classroom

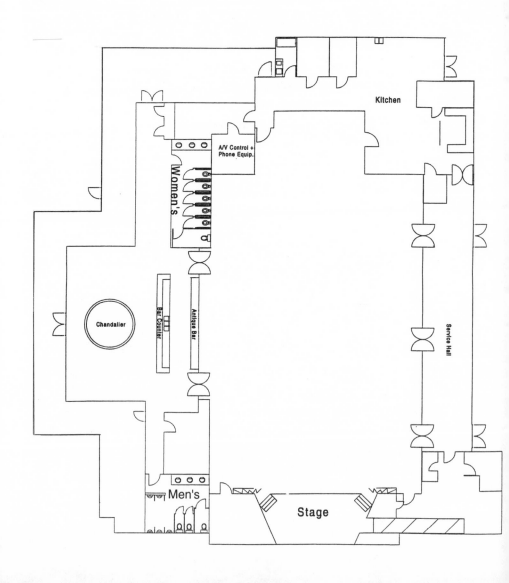

The Settlement House

Close your eyes. Can you hear the clink of spurs and the thump of booted feet as the doors swing open and a posse of cowpokes crowds up to the mirrored elegance of the bar? It's all here: livery stable, hotel, saloon ... even that necessary frontier accommodation, the jail.

Sam's Place

Rooms, Specifications, Capacities & Seating Styles:

Breakout I
    300 sq. ft. (15 x 20)
    8 - Conference

Breakout II
    300 sq. ft. (15 x 20)
    8 - Conference

Main Room
    288 sq. ft. (16 x 18)
    10 - Conference

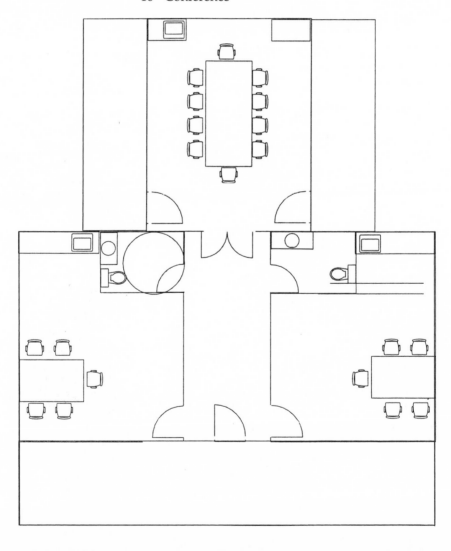

Sam's Place

The classic simplicity of this small building represents the best of early Texas architecture, so we named it for a man who would have felt right at home on its wide front porch ... Sam Houston.

Old Sam would have been proud.

La Hacienda

Rooms, Specifications, Capacities & Seating Styles:

Sleeping Rooms: 19

Conquistador
- 1,296 sq. ft. (48 x 27)
- 183 - Reception
- 90 - Theater
- 80 - Banquet
- 64 - Classroom
- 38 - Hollow Square
- 32 - U Shape
- 26 - Conference

Durango
- 500 sq. ft. (20 x 25)
- 39 - Reception
- 30 - Theater
- 24 - Banquet
- 20 - Hollow Square
- 20 - Classroom
- 16 - U Shape
- 12 - Conference

Chairman's Boardroom
- 750 sq. ft. (30 x 25)
- 14 - Conference

Executive Boardroom
- 352 sq. ft. (22 x 16)
- 10 - Conference

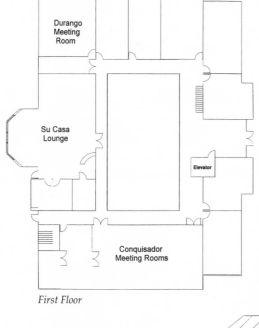

First Floor

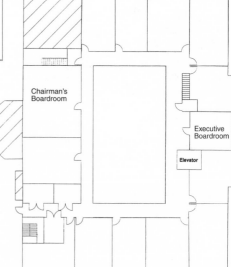

Second Floor

La Hacienda

As an event-space with Spanish atmosphere, La Hacienda is a popular meeting site. It features a comfortable lounge, conference rooms, accommodation for overnight guests and a courtyard with a fountain and a cloistered walk.

La Hacienda, true Southwestern hospitality: Mi casa es su casa … my house is your house.

Footsteps of Heroes

Historians tell that General Sam Houston and his band of volunteers marched across this land on their way to San Jacinto. A commemorative marker invites you to take a walk through the trees ... In the Footsteps of Heroes.

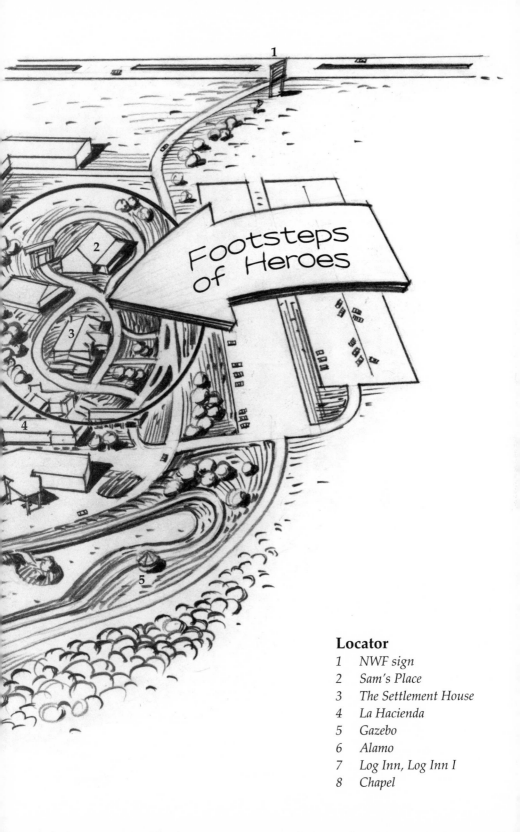

Footsteps of Heroes

Locator
1 NWF sign
2 Sam's Place
3 The Settlement House
4 La Hacienda
5 Gazebo
6 Alamo
7 Log Inn, Log Inn I
8 Chapel

The Log Inns

Rooms, Specifications, Capacities & Seating Styles:

Log Inn I
15 - Sleeping Rooms

Log Inn
1,845 (45 x 41)
264 - Reception
78 - Banquet

Log Inn Banquet Room
437 sq. ft. (23 x 19)
62 - Reception
28 - Theater
24 - Banquet
24 - Classroom
20 - Hollow Square
16 - U Shape
12 - Conference

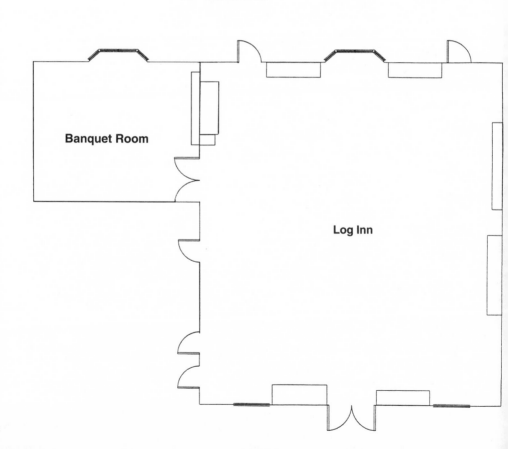

The Log Inn I

Old ways are best. When our pioneer fore-fathers pushed their way into the wilderness they used logs hewn from the surrounding forest to build their sturdy homes. Gather 'round the fireplace on a cold winter evening and appreciate the enduring comfort of the Log Inn.

Town Hall

Specifications:

2,880 sq. ft.

Capacity & Seating Styles:

72 - Boardroom
240 - Theater
144 - Banquet
100 - Classroom

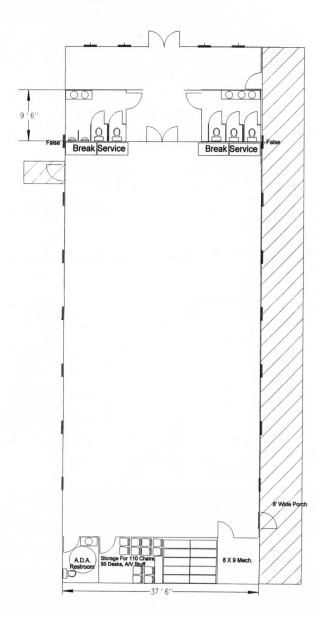

Town Hall

This was the center of community life in the late 1800's. Step out onto the large patio of our Town Hall, and listen to our authentic schoolhouse bell. You'll dream of days gone by.

The Gazebo

Ducks paddle in the shallows and a squirrel frisks fearlessly on a nearby limb. As the sun peeps over the horizon, the mist that hides the lake becomes as luminous as the inside of a pearl.

The Gazebo is the perfect setting for photo shoots, small weddings and small parties.

The Chapel

Are you planning a wedding? Ancient vows take on a new and deeper meaning when repeated in this tiny building, an oasis of serenity set among a riot of flowers.

Ideal for photo shoots and small weddings.

The Colony

Secluded under tall pines, this cluster of cabins reminds one of the nice lady's boarding house from the old TV westerns. It has just the right "at home" feel, with beautiful decor and stone fireplaces. In fact, we even named each cabin – Aunt Pitty Pat's, Fishing Hole, Picket Fence and others.